Praise for Lisa Sasevi[...]

MEANT FOR M[...]

"You can make a difference with what you already know and make great money doing it. Grab this inspiring book today!"

— Jeff Walker, *New York Times* bestselling author of *Launch*

"A must-read! Lisa has unlocked the proven formula to be paid what you're worth."

— Kevin Harrington, The Original Shark from ABC's *Shark Tank*

"In this profound book, Lisa Sasevich systematically outlines the steps to unlock your genius and live a life of greater abundance and contribution. Lisa is a master who has transformed thousands of people's lives—including my own."

— Jack Canfield, co-creator of the Chicken Soup for the Soul series

"Required reading for heart-centered entrepreneurs, speakers, authors, coaches and consultants. Sasevich makes the unsavory , parts of business not only doable, but easy."

— JJ Virgin, *New York Times* bestselling author of *The Virgin Diet* and founder of The Mindshare Summit

"Powerful stuff. I wish I'd had Lisa's incredible system when I first got started over 30 years ago. It would have cut years off my success journey and saved me a fortune in mistakes. Her brilliant system has added an extra zero to my income."

— Robert Allen, *New York Times* bestselling author, writer of many best-selling books including *Nothing Down*, *Multiple Streams of Income* and *The One Minute Millionaire*

"I've learned much from [Lisa's] wit and wisdom and you will too. Her proven track record for transforming lives speaks volumes and so does this fabulous book. Share it with your most valued friends and they will thank you."

— Marcia Wieder, Founder/CEO of Dream University

MEANT FOR␣MORE

THE PROVEN FORMULA
TO TURN YOUR
KNOWLEDGE INTO PROFITS

LISA SASEVICH

HAY HOUSE

HAY HOUSE

Carlsbad, California • New York City
London • Sydney • New Delhi

Published in the United Kingdom by:
Hay House UK Ltd, The Sixth Floor, Watson House,
54 Baker Street, London W1U 7BU
Tel: +44 (0)20 3927 7290; Fax: +44 (0)20 3927 7291; www.hayhouse.co.uk

Published in the United States of America by:
Hay House Inc., PO Box 5100, Carlsbad, CA 92018-5100
Tel: (1) 760 431 7695 or (800) 654 5126
Fax: (1) 760 431 6948 or (800) 650 5115; www.hayhouse.com

Published in Australia by:
Hay House Australia Ltd, 18/36 Ralph St, Alexandria NSW 2015
Tel: (61) 2 9669 4299; Fax: (61) 2 9669 4144; www.hayhouse.com.au

Published in India by:
Hay House Publishers India, Muskaan Complex, Plot No.3, B-2,
Vasant Kunj, New Delhi 110 070
Tel: (91) 11 4176 1620; Fax: (91) 11 4176 1630; www.hayhouse.co.in

Text © Lisa Sasevich, 2020

Cover design: Charles McStravick • *Interior design:* Bryn Starr Best

A catalogue record for this book is available from the British Library.

Tradepaper ISBN: 978-1-78817-082-6
Hardback ISBN: 978-1-4019-5544-1
E-book ISBN: 978-1-4019-5545-8
Audiobook ISBN: 978-1-4019-5547-2

Printed and bound by CPI Group (UK) Ltd, Croydon, CR0 4YY

To Elijah and Sierra,

May God bless you with

health, wealth, and the

happiness that comes

with knowing you make

a difference in the world.

I love you with all my heart.

~ Mom

CONTENTS

INTRODUCTION

THAT FEELING THAT WON'T GO AWAY

When I was 19, my mom died in my arms after a yearlong battle with lung cancer. She was 47. I remember the day of her memorial service in our backyard: the awkwardness of people not knowing what to say, the pit in my stomach whenever I touched the reality that she was really gone, the look of devastation on people's faces when they saw me. But what I remember most of all is what I overheard people saying about my mother. They spoke about what a caring and dynamic person she was, always so full of life and the first one to raise her hand to volunteer or help an important cause. And right on the heels of that, they slipped in their thoughts about how well she could have done had she left her job and started her own business.

My mom had worked full-time for a big aerospace company, designing the many forms they needed on her drafting table (this was in the days before desktop computing and graphic design software). She always had some kind of side hustle, whether it was helping small businesses with their design needs or selling stuffed animals to her coworkers and then donating the money to a local shelter for domestic abuse survivors. As they recalled my mom's efforts, her friends said that if only she had taken a chance a little sooner, had more confidence, and realized how special she was, she could have used her gifts to do even more in the world.

While it hurt to hear these words, I knew these people who loved my mom were right—the light behind her eyes had gone out even before she had gotten sick. At that moment, I realized one thing: She had been meant for more. Her friends knew it. Her family knew it. All the small business owners and charities she helped knew it. And even at my young age, I knew it. Devastatingly, it was too late for her.

My dad, on the other hand, had owned his gifts in a much more public way. He was a member of a band in Miami Beach, Florida, during the Latin craze. He loved performing, playing music, and helping people have a good time, but when he found out that while he was making a hundred bucks a week, the opening comedian playing the same gig on the same tour was making a grand a week, he felt called to step up his game. So he taught himself ventriloquism, developed an act where his dummy, Chico Chico, would pop out of his conga drum and start cracking jokes, and moved from the back of the stage to front and center. Why? He could sense that he was being called to use that knack for entertaining in a bigger way. It wasn't just the money; he knew, probably like you do, that he was meant for more.

Comparing his life to my mom's (they had divorced when I was three) made my mom's death even more poignant.

When my mom died, I realized that I had a choice. I, too, could live a life that would end with my friends lamenting how I "could have, would have, should have" unwrapped my gifts and made more of myself. Or I could figure out how to live my purpose, use my God-given gifts, and do something meaningful, and hopefully lucrative too. It was also abundantly clear that none of us knows how long we have. If I wanted to have a life of meaning, it was time to stop playing small. After all, this life, right now, is not a dress rehearsal. It's the real prime-time show!

Because you've picked up this book, I know you've got it— that gnawing feeling that deep down you know you are capable of being more, creating more, making more of a difference in the world and being recognized for it, which, in many cases, leads to having more, if only you knew how. It's the kind of feeling that, no matter how much you ignore it or try to stuff it down, keeps coming back up. It simply won't go away.

I know the automatic tendency is to shut down this internal voice with thoughts like, *Who am I to think I can be more? I'm truly blessed, so why can't I just be content with what I've got? And what if I put myself out there only to waste my time or worse . . . make a fool of myself?*

Longing for a bigger, more purposeful and abundant kind of life isn't something to feel bad about. That feeling that you were meant for more is a gift. It's a calling for you to grow. And we're really only happy when we're growing.

OPENING THE DOOR TO "MORE"

As clear as that feeling of being meant for more is, it's not an easy one to act on. It can be overwhelming to know you are meant for more and yet be unsure of what that "more" is or how to make it happen. If you have a hidden belief—as so many of us do—that in order to be successful you have to give up something important, like your integrity, your quirkiness, or time with your family, it can stop you in your tracks. And it can be demoralizing to look around and see people with a weaker work ethic and less talent and heart getting ahead simply because they seem to have a knack for talking themselves up to the right people.

The bridge between feeling you are meant for more and making that more come true is putting yourself out there, whether that means starting a business, marketing the one you already have, or sharing your ideas in a bigger way. And any of these things requires some form of selling—something most people are resistant to.

I know what you might be thinking. *Do I have to tell people about myself and my work? Can't I just build it and they will come? Or envision it and it will happen? Isn't there some way to skip the sales part?* The simple answer is no. No, you can't leave your gifts, your impact, and your happiness—as well as the gifts, impact, and happiness of others—up to chance. Well, you can, but it essentially keeps your gifts a secret and your rewards elusive. And I'm guessing you already know how frustrating that is.

I know that the very thought of selling yourself can bring up all kinds of negative associations—a smarmy used-car salesman, or scripted telemarketer, or aggressive perfume sales clerk who follows you around the mall. But I have been in sales for over 30 years, and I can tell you there is a bigger, more loving way to look at selling that is every bit as real as these stereotypes.

Whether you're pitching an idea to your kids, advice to a friend, a career change to your spouse, or a product or service to a potential client, sales is about creating an opportunity for transformation. It's about seeking the greatest good for everyone involved—you and the person you're seeking a yes from. It's *not* about manipulating people, pushing, or winning.

Ultimately, sales is about helping people say yes to themselves.

I believe in the power of sales to improve lives so much that I have created the Meant for More Formula to help you do it too. Since 2009, I've had the honor of teaching mission-driven entrepreneurs, experts, and service professionals how to get out there and make the difference—and the money—they were put here to make by learning how to claim their gifts, know their worth, and sell without being sales-y. My graduates live in 134 countries. Collectively, we estimate that they've made more than $375 million helping people with their gifts, talents, and expertise, using the principles I teach.

My team and I work with people who are either in business for themselves or seriously considering launching their own ventures. They typically fall into two categories:

- New business owners looking for clear steps to increase sales
- Established coaches, authors, experts, and service professionals who want to take their business to the next level

While the Meant for More Formula is specifically designed for entrepreneurs, it also works if you're trying to make the most of a corporate job, if you're in transition from working for a company to creating your own thing, or if you're a stay-at-home parent or retiree in search of that second-half career or seeking to up your impact through volunteering. Basically, it applies to anyone with that feeling that won't go away—the feeling that there is something more you're meant to do with your time here on earth. Everything I teach about how to grow your business is also directly applicable to growing your life. My clients consistently report that they've used the strategies contained in the Meant for More Formula, as I have, to inspire their kids, spouses, family members, and friends to reach for their own versions of more.

One of my clients, Kathryn, is married to a great guy—a musician—and they have two young daughters. When I met her, Kathryn was the primary breadwinner, supporting her husband's dream of playing music professionally by working as a freelance copywriter. Kathryn was good at what she did—so good that one client came to rely on her more and more until she eventually offered to make Kathryn a partner. That's how Kathryn came to be at my event, as a "plus one" to this client. When we got to the segment of the training where I teach about being meant for more, Kathryn had a realization that she wasn't happy. Although she loved her husband and her daughters, Kathryn wanted to hit the snooze button every day because her life felt consumed by work and motherhood. It was all obligation, no passion. In that moment of clarity, Kathryn also realized that she didn't want to build someone else's dream, and that she wasn't going to accept the partnership her client was offering.

After the training, Kathryn began to see that she had a knack for figuring out the technical side of business—she was always helping her copywriting clients update their websites or figure out their e-mail newsletter service. Once Kathryn started to do more of the "techy" work that she enjoyed and that came naturally to her, she quickly got enough business to stop working with her copywriting clients. Yet it wasn't the money that made the biggest impact on her life. It was that she couldn't wait to get out of bed in the morning and get to work. As a result, she could be more present with her kids because she didn't have to try to make them her main source of fulfillment. She didn't resent her husband's pursuit of his dream, because she was going after hers too, and now their relationship is stronger than ever (which is saying something for a couple with two kids under three in the house).

This is the kind of ripple effect that happens when you start advocating for yourself and getting out there with what I call your "irresistible offer" (whether money ever changes hands or not). An irresistible offer is exactly what it sounds like: an invitation that is so compelling and on point that the person it's intended for can't help but say yes. There are three main components of an irresistible offer, which we'll cover in Chapter 10, but at this point all you need to know is that you are about to learn how to make offers that will have others pursuing your gifts, talents, services, and advice—you won't have to chase anyone down. With the structures that you'll learn on these pages, you'll know exactly how to present your offer so that the structures do the selling for you—all you have to do is show up and be yourself. Remember how Bugs Bunny would smell a roast turkey in the next room and start floating through the air toward it? With irresistible offers, it's like you become the turkey, and the people you're meant to help float toward you on the delicious vibes you're putting out.

At its heart, this book is about leadership. I define leadership as knowing how to give people what they need to make a decision and say yes to themselves. My intention is that reading this book will empower you to step out as a leader in your family, relationships, work, community, and in your own life—not in an ego-based way, but in a way that is generous, courageous, and compassionate. Generous because you want to help others give themselves a chance to make the difference you know they're capable of making. Compassionate in being able to look out beyond your own life and love another person enough to see that they are meant for more and offer them a new possibility. And courageous in that you are willing to put yourself forward as someone who has the power to help others. Because you do. Every single one of you reading this does, right now. It's already inside of you and ready to be unveiled.

I want reading this book to help you tap into the confidence that people need you, that you're worthy, and that this longing for "more" is a seed that is ripening at this moment for a reason.

What prevents so many people from owning their gifts and using them to make a difference is the challenge of figuring out how to take this intangible thing and make it visible to others— how to communicate it in such a way that they inspire not just excitement but actual commitment from people they are capable of helping. That's why this book is full of exercises, ideas, mind-set breakthroughs, and step-by-step processes. The Meant for More Formula has been tried and tested by me as well as by over 15,000 students of ours all over the world. Everything you're holding in your hand has been implemented by others just like you. This guide will help you unwrap your gift, develop the courage to own it, and inspire you to offer it to others generously and with compassion.

THE TRAINING CAMP WHERE I HONED MY SALES SKILLS

I wrote this book because I know firsthand the pain of *not* living up to your potential and knowing that there must be something more available to you. I spent decades with this feeling, and now I want to share everything I've learned with you so that you don't have to wait that long to start reframing the game and making the impact you were meant to make.

I wish I could say that my mom dying got me to figure everything out right away, but I had more blessings disguised as heartbreaks coming.

Fueled by a desire to make the most of my life, I hustled to finish college early. After graduation, I went to work in sales at some of the biggest companies in America, including Pfizer and Hewlett-Packard. I became a top sales performer wherever I went, because I came factory installed with a knack for selling and a desire to keep learning and upping my game. A true results junkie, I would keep toying with a process until I got the outcome I desired. Yet, despite the fact that I was killing it at work, there was always something missing.

I was living a double life: weekdays I was consistently growing revenue by four and sometimes five hundred percent, nights and weekends I was poring over self-help books and attending personal development seminars. I knew there had to be something more meaningful and rewarding for me than selling Viagra or printers. But the money I was earning on the job made it hard to leave. The fact that the money was also supporting my then-husband and me as he attended medical school made it seem nearly impossible to quit a salaried job.

And then one of the seminars I attended changed my life. This particular course taught women how to create powerful partnerships with the men in their lives. The things I learned there made a huge difference in my relationship. I loved it so much and got so much value out of it, in fact, that I left corporate America to help grow that business. I felt like I had found my calling! I wanted every woman in the world to know about this work. I felt I had discovered a powerful tool, and it felt selfish to keep it to myself. Even better, I loved the woman who ran the company. She was more than a boss to me. She was a mentor.

I started with this company by leading their free evening workshops where I packed as much useful content as I could into three hours and then made an offer for the women attending to buy a weekend-long seminar. I knew that if a woman showed up to the introductory workshop, she was open to learning something new and that I had one chance to get her to decide if she wanted to learn more. If she left without signing up for the seminar, I knew she probably never would.

Because I believed in what I was teaching so wholeheartedly, if I led an intro workshop and 30 percent of the women signed up for the weekend seminar—which I would later find out is a pretty great conversion rate—I would go back to my hotel room and cry about the 70 percent who didn't register. I was determined to figure out what I could do to get more women to say yes to themselves on the spot, while they were with me at the intro event and were open to a new possibility. I played with every variable I could: the chair arrangements, the lighting, the length of the breaks, how much I encouraged discussion versus how much time I spent teaching, price points, bonuses, you name it. Eventually I got to a point where as many as 60 percent of the women who attended my introductory workshops signed up for a $500 weekend. And I regularly had as many as 85 percent of the women attending the first weekend course go on to enroll in more advanced seminars with us.

I had no idea that in the outside world, getting 10 percent of people to act on an offer on the spot was considered a major success. I was so focused on serving those women in the room that I was in a bubble and didn't realize that the results I was getting were, well . . . off the charts!

After six years with the company, during which I grew the business from $300,000 a year to $1.3 million, my bubble burst. I got fired. It was the night before Christmas Eve. It felt like my calling had hung up on me. After the death of my mom when I was 19, it was the most painful thing that had ever happened to me. Yet it came with a major blessing—eventually it became clear that my calling had grown, just as my dad's had when he transitioned out of playing with the band to being a front-and-center one-man act. This is what happens when you accept that you are meant for more—or, as in my case, when the universe gives you a nudge to show you that you are. Periodically, your view of what you're intended to do will evolve. The pieces of what you believed to be your unique gift will rearrange themselves and you'll be able to use those same gifts in a more expanded way. In my case, after being fired from my dream job, I knew for sure that I didn't want to grow anyone else's business again. It was time for me to step out on my own as an entrepreneur and use my innate and well-honed gift for sales to grow my own bottom line. The problem? I had no clue what I would be offering.

I went on a search to figure out what product or service I could create and sell. I started attending seminars, reading books, and working with a coach. It was in my very first session that my coach asked me where I shined and what really made my heart sing. I told him how I was good at helping companies grow. When I told him I consistently had 30, 60, and even 85 percent of people saying yes to my offers on the spot, he immediately said, "Lisa, wait, stop! I know what your unique value is." Even though I had built so many other people's businesses, I couldn't see that making irresistible offers was my strength. It had all felt so easy that I didn't think twice about it. And I certainly didn't realize it was something I could make big money doing—and make a big difference teaching others how to do.

(By the way, everybody has abilities, gifts, and talents that come so naturally to them that they are tough for them to see. This book will help you discover yours.)

I wrote down all the things I had figured out about making offers that inspired people to say yes on the spot—what to say and what not to say, how to inspire action, when to use incentives, and, just as importantly, what I *never* did, because it felt wrong or slimy. That's where my business, The Invisible Close, was birthed. It turns out that those six years I spent building someone else's dream had been the perfect training camp for defining my unique abilities to sell without being sales-y, which eventually became the foundation of my own business and the way I would make a huge difference for thousands of people all over the world. (You too have been in the perfect training camp to hone the gifts that will help you reach for your version of "more"—we'll uncover that as well.)

I started offering my coaching and advice to people one-on-one for an hourly fee. I quickly got so busy that I maxed out (which is common when you land on the thing that you are uniquely suited to help others with). While it was amazing to be busy and in demand, every additional hour I could have worked would have meant an hour less with my kids, or a missed workout, or a cancelled date night with my then-husband. So I learned to leverage the power of speaking to small groups and using the internet to attract clients, which allowed me to make my offer to more than one person at a time and also to serve more than one person at a time. This is referred to as leveraging yourself and your time.

I have made a very good living distilling powerful concepts into easy-to-follow systems. We've been named to the *Inc.* 500—a list of the fastest-growing privately held companies in the United States—two years in a row. We were number 20 on the list of woman-owned businesses and the number two training company in San Diego. Also, as a result of the massive boost to my income that came from tapping into my gifts and following my calling to expand, I've been able to fulfill a lifelong dream and become an active philanthropist, having personally raised and donated over $1 million for organizations including the Just Like My Child Foundation, the eWomenNetwork Foundation, Global Dental Relief, and Natural High. I've also received the coveted eWomenNetwork Foundation Champion award and Donor of the Year Award from the Just Like My Child Foundation for my fundraising efforts. I am living proof that the systems I teach work, and they have benefited not just me—they have dramatically improved the lives of the people I care about too.

THE KEY TO BRINGING YOUR VERSION OF "MORE" TO LIFE

The most important step you can take is simply deciding it's time to act. Because here's a fundamental truth:

> *Transformation doesn't happen without a decision. Really, that's what sales is all about at its core: helping others make a decision. And you can't do that if you haven't decided for yourself that you want to reach for your personal definition of "more."*

That's what I've designed this book to help you do—to decide that you are going to say yes to yourself, start acting on that feeling that won't go away, and pursue your purpose. I know it might sound scary and like a lot of work, but the great news is that all it takes to reach for your "meant for more" is getting clear on the value you offer and shifting the way you think about sales. Once you've opened your mind to what's possible, you can use the proven structures I outline in this book to support your success.

I have spent the past two decades developing the Meant for More Formula, which systematizes simple mind-set shifts and practical strategies and helps you reliably create transformation for yourself and for others. When you use the formula to start crafting irresistible offers, you invite more freedom and rewards into your life, and into the lives of the people you help, whether they are your kids, friends, partner, family, or clients. In other words, you show the universe that you mean business. That's when unseen forces come to your aid. I've personally experienced this and been witness to this kind of invisible assistance helping thousands of mission-driven go-getters—and all they had to do to jump-start this process was make a decision to start on the journey to more.

The Meant for More Formula is for you if:

- You know deep down inside that you have so much more to offer the world.

- You feel like there's something standing between you and greater success and fulfillment.

- You have years of experience in your field and you want to help others who are just starting out.

- You've cracked the code on something others struggle with, and you want to help others with what you've learned.

- You're tired of being the best-kept secret in your field.

- You're already in business for yourself and people love you . . . but they rarely buy from you.

This proven formula teaches you how to sell yourself and your one-of-a-kind gifts to the people you were meant to help and reap the rewards that come when you stop giving away your gifts for free—and to do it in a way that isn't remotely sales-y, pushy, or icky.

If you take the ideas in this book to heart, rewire your thinking, and implement these systems, it's like flipping a switch—knowing the Meant for More Formula will help erase any traces of fear or distaste of selling right out of your mind. Suddenly, making your offer to people becomes an honorable thing to do. Something you do without any angst or dread. Something you even look forward to, because you can simply let the structures I teach do the selling for you, while you get to be your authentic, heartfelt, generous self.

THE IMPORTANCE OF STRUCTURE

In the course of my career, whether I was growing someone else's business or my own, I have come to see that success isn't about luck or even talent. It's about discovering a system that reliably produces favorable results for everyone involved, and then surrendering to that system. You may hear the word "system" and inwardly shudder because it sounds so . . . formulaic. Perhaps even boring. But a system merely provides a framework. The system shows you the steps, but it doesn't control how you implement or deliver on those steps. It's not a script. It's a structure. And something my clients hear me say again and again is that structure gives you freedom.

Giving you freedom to make the difference you know deep down you were put here to make is the aim of the structure that is the Meant for More Formula. With it, you always know what to do next, but you get to bring your own flair, personality, and point of view to how you do it. And that is no small thing, because that is how you sell without being sales-y. Pouring your individuality and great work into my proven structures allows you to simply show up, be yourself, and make the difference you were put here to make—while you reap the rewards that come as a natural response to doing good in the world.

We are all seeking structure, whether we're aware of it or not. The world is a chaotic place, and structure helps us feel safe as it also carves out a path to wherever it is we want to go. Even people who quit their corporate jobs because they don't want to be chained to their desks for eight hours a day will find themselves sitting at the desk in their home office from 9 to 5 if they don't give themselves an alternate structure to their day—that's how much we all unconsciously gravitate toward structure. That's why I created the Meant for More Formula, so that you could have a structure that helps you create a reality that suits you and your unique gifts and dreams instead of submitting to a default structure of doing something you don't particularly like just to pay the bills.

The structure of this book follows the structure of the Meant for More Formula. Each step of the formula gets its own section:

- **Step One: Reframe the Game and Make Peace with Sales**

    In this vital first step, you upgrade your mind-set to get on board with the idea of selling and to get inspired by the many wonderful things that your knowing how to sell (without being sales-y, of course) makes possible for yourself and others.

- **Step Two: Claim Your Gifts**

    Once you've opened your mind to thinking differently, it's time to find and claim your superpowers, or what I call your unique value, so that you can start consciously using them to create new results for yourself and the people you can help the most. Discovering your unique value is the key to stepping into your "meant for more" life!

- **Step Three: Get into Action**

  Discovering your unique value so you can claim your gifts is game changing, but only if you do something with it. It's easy to keep yourself busy, but I want to make sure you have forward momentum! Here you will learn the simple yet powerful secrets that will transform your insight into action and propel you and your mission forward.

- **Step Four: Invite Pursuit with Your Irresistible Offer**

  Next, you learn how to make your invitation in a way that inspires others into action—no pushing, manipulating, or smarmy sales techniques required. This is when others start pursuing you for those skills and talents that only you have, and that is a wonderful feeling!

  Best of all, you learn how to make your offer in any type of setting, whether that's one-on-one, in interviews (such as on a blog or podcast), at a live event (whether that's from a stage, at a small networking meeting, or in a workshop you're leading), or online. Whatever situation you find yourself in, the structure of knowing how to craft and make an irresistible offer will have you covered!

- **Step Five: Live Your "More"**

  Finally, we cover the structures that will help you continue to consistently offer your gifts, advice, and/or services and get what you're worth, no matter what's going on in your personal life or the world at large. These techniques are how you stop backsliding into an old structure that no longer serves you and make your new reality as a person who is making a big difference in the world.

In every step of the formula, I include practical exercises you can use right away in your own life and business. You don't have to wait until you've finished the book to start using them. In fact, please don't! Doing the exercises even when you still feel unclear will help you find the clarity and confidence that you've been looking for. Once you try something new, you become a new person who can see new possibilities, and why would you want to wait to create those new possibilities for yourself? You can always refine as you go (a concept you'll learn more about in Chapter 8, "Get Past Perfection"). To make it even easier, I've compiled a guide to all the exercises in this book in one place that you can access at www.MeantForMoreGuide.com, along with additional resources to help you take what you're learning here even further.

Throughout the book I also include stories from clients as well as my own life to show you all the various ways the structures I teach can be applied. My clients inspire me every day with their openness, their gifts, and their successes, and I trust they will inspire you too and open your mind to new ways of creating abundance that you may have never thought of.

Once you learn the principles of the Meant for More Formula, you'll start to see them and be able to apply them everywhere—none of them are terribly technical or require a rocket-scientist IQ or a heaping helping of innate charisma to pull off. These are simple secrets that are all around you. Yet unless you've been clued in, they're sort of hiding in plain sight—that's why I named my business The Invisible Close. When you learn to recognize them and then put them to use in your own life, you'll stop feeling like you're spinning your wheels and start zooming toward what you want. Even better, the things you want will start moving to meet you because you exert a powerful gravitational pull—what I call "invisible influence." That's when friends, romantic partners, clients, and opportunities start pursuing you. And it's a cycle that just keeps building. The more you learn how to sell yourself and your ideas, and the more you refine your mind-set, the more momentum you build.

And if, like me or thousands of my clients, you get inspired to turn your calling for more into a moneymaking venture that helps others, that's exactly what my business, The Invisible Close, can teach you to do. We have heaps of free resources, as well as paid programs, at www.LisaSasevich.com that can help you turn the thing you care about the most and that comes the easiest to you into a successful business. So if you, like Kathryn, whose story I shared earlier in this introduction, realize that you want to get paid handsomely to help people by doing what comes naturally to you, we've got you covered!

I'm so excited to share this system with you. After all, I'm a Jewish mother! Meaning, unless you are fed, nourished, and totally taken care of, I can't relax. That's another one of my gifts. And now I can't wait to help you unwrap yours.

STEP ONE

REFRAME THE GAME AND MAKE PEACE WITH SALES

Here is a simple truth: The only tool you need to get from where you are now and where you know in your heart you are ready to be is the ability to sell yourself, your ideas, your knowledge, your service, or your advice. It doesn't matter how smart, talented, or passionate you are; if you don't ever open up and make an offer that gets the people around you into action and saying yes—because you don't want to seem too pushy—you'll go through life trying to find contentment from whatever happens to land in your lap. It's like lying on the ground with your mouth open, waiting for rain to fall into your mouth instead of getting yourself a glass of water; at some point, you're going to get awfully thirsty. And, my friend, you were not put on this earth to slowly die of dehydration.

In this first step of the Meant for More Formula, you're going to rewire any negative thoughts or associations you may have about selling and write a new definition of sales for yourself. This is the most internal step of the formula, because it's about changing your mind-set, but it's a vital piece. When you can get excited about selling with both your mind and your heart (and yes, it is possible!), doors that were previously closed will open to you, and you'll be able to waltz through them while wondering why they seemed so impenetrable before. Whether you're seeking more money, more clients, more influence, more fulfillment, or to make more of a difference, the key to your goals lies within this step.

CHAPTER 1

WAKE UP, MY FRIEND, WE'RE ALL SELLING SOMETHING

It's the end of the school year, and the elementary school auditorium is packed with proud families. We're all here for the choir recital—every member of the audience has a kid who loves to sing so much that they've shown up at 7 A.M. twice a week for the last nine months to study and practice with Miss Julie, the beloved choir teacher. (My daughter is one of them.) It's the culmination of a lot of hard work, and everyone in the room is feeling the energy—the kids sing their hearts out, and we in the audience are lapping it up. After the final song, many kids are crying because they don't want choir to end.

Miss Julie gets up after the program to thank the kids and the families. Some of the kids give her roses, and then everyone starts gathering their things and filing out of the auditorium. It's a beautiful moment—one that could be even better if there wasn't something very important missing.

You see, Miss Julie offers a summer program—she's sent home flyers in the kids' backpacks once or twice in the past few weeks. I've been meaning to sign my daughter up for the summer session, but the flyers are lost in the stack of paperwork that comes home around the end of the school year. I know my daughter loves those summer classes, and I love that she keeps up with her singing. Today would be the perfect opportunity for me to be able to sign her up and leave knowing that that particular open loop is now closed. In that moment, a whopping majority of parents would sign their kids up for that summer program if it were easy for them to do so. Sadly, Miss Julie's completely forgotten to mention it while she has us there.

This, of course, is killing me, because this is what I teach people how to do—make offers that inspire people to take on-the-spot action on something that's calling to them. I pull Miss Julie aside and say, "Don't you want to tell us about the summer program?"

At that moment, a light goes off in Miss Julie's eyes and she races to get the microphone. It's already been turned off, so she has to scramble all the way to the back of the crowded auditorium to get it turned back on. Then she shouts into the microphone, "Don't forget to sign up for the summer program—you should have the form already at home." By this time, half the families have already left. Now Miss Julie will have to do the part of her job that she hates the most: the sales part. This means she'll have to start sending out a bunch of e-mails and making calls to parents, reminding them to sign up and tell friends who might be interested. And now the parents will have to dig through that stack of papers and try to find the form, plus field e-mails from Miss Julie. And the kids have a smaller chance of getting to do something they love that summer. And in the middle of all of this, year after year, Miss Julie is always mystified by how much work it takes to fill her program given how many rabid and loyal fans she has. Sound familiar?

With just a tiny bit of forethought, Miss Julie could have placed a flyer and a pen on everyone's chair, had one or two of the kids who have done the summer program in the past stand up to say how great it was, and then offered an enticing, easy-to-fulfill bonus for parents who signed up that day on the spot, whether it was a T-shirt or a solo at the next recital or even a free video of today's recital, since she was filming it anyway, then told us where to hand in the completed form before we left. With just a smidge of reverse engineering on Miss Julie's part to come up with an offer that was irresistible, she would have freed herself from pursuing people to get them to sign up. And she could put all that energy into serving, which she loves to do, instead of spending the first half of summer feeling like she's pushing and selling.

Or take the temple where my family and I attend services. This is not a pass-the-basket-every-Sunday kind of place. They do a fundraising ask exactly once a year in which various people tell deep and moving stories about how the temple has impacted their lives. This happens just before they pass out envelopes. The problem is, they don't remind us to bring our checkbooks in advance. They don't tell us what to do with the envelope in the event that we've miraculously remembered to bring our checkbooks and have a pen with us. I've left with the check in my hand before, and I know I'm not the only one. In fact, I remember once trying to slide it under the temple office door because I just didn't know where to put the darn thing! Then it's on us to mail the checks to the temple, which sometimes we'll do and sometimes we won't. They could easily triple the amount of money they raise each year simply by making it easier for us to give them money. And with triple the money, they could have triple the impact with the outreach and education programs they are seeking to fund.

Miss Julie's a teacher. My rabbi is a religious leader. They both probably think that, given their professions, they don't have to know how to sell. Yet their lives could be so much easier, and their work could be so much more impactful to so many more people, if they put just a little more thought into their offer and made it easier for people to say yes to them.

Because they have an aversion to anything remotely resembling selling, they make their lives exponentially harder and their impact decidedly smaller. If you have any kind of resistance to sales, you are doing the same thing. It doesn't have to be this way!

When you know the structures that help you sell—which I will walk you through in detail in Step Four of the Meant for More Formula later in this book—you'll see that they are so easy it's just silly not to do them. When you implement these systems, all you need to do at any given time is stay present in the moment and be yourself. You don't have to fake it, turn into a salesperson, or learn how to manipulate people. The structure does the selling for you.

But there is one step that comes first. And this first step is often the hardest one—changing your mind-set about sales and acknowledging that it's your responsibility to make offers to the people you're meant to serve.

If you aren't at peace with the concept of selling, it doesn't matter how many techniques you have in your back pocket, because you're going to forget to make your offer, just like Miss Julie did. Or you'll do it in such a discreet way that people may not even realize you're offering them something, which is what happened with my rabbi's fundraising efforts. Either way, your path is going to feel a lot more arduous, and your results are going to be limited. Perhaps you'll even give up and go back to settling for whatever life hands you. And then the people you're meant to help won't get your assistance. It's a lose-lose situation. Meaning, it's truly a disservice not to make your offer.

ALL THE DIFFERENT WAYS YOU ARE SELLING ALL DAY, EVERY DAY

Making peace with selling is also important because, whether you realize it or not, you are already doing it in every part of your life. All of the following daily activities are actually types of selling—even though you may not yet see them that way:

- Getting kids to get ready for school, do their homework, help out around the house, and go to bed

- Making travel plans with your girlfriends
- Pitching your partner on an idea, whether it's something big, like a move, or small, like making a plan to go out on a date
- Enrolling a homeowner in recurring weekly or monthly service
- Sharing your ideas in a meeting, e-mail, or presentation
- Offering advice to a friend
- Coordinating a volunteer effort
- Pitching a potential client
- Getting buy-in from your boss
- Encouraging a patient to take the next step
- Having a tough conversation with a loved one
- Teaching your kids something important
- Getting to know someone new at a cocktail party or networking event
- Any area in which you want to persuade someone to get into action or see something your way

All these scenarios require selling. What they *don't* require is being pushy and manipulative or trying to get one over on someone else. This is an important idea to get into your head, because the number one resistance I see from people who haven't made peace with sales is that selling somehow seems underhanded, self-serving, perhaps even evil. The tape most people have playing in their heads about sales revolves around the idea that sales is a battle; and the person who is doing the selling is seeking to win, which means that if you say yes to the pitch, you lose. In the used-car salesman scenario, the car lot profits and the buyer gets stuck with the lemon. The company wins and the little guy loses. And sales is nothing more than a tactic to separate you from your money.

7

There is a much more empowering way to define sales, which we'll get to in just a moment. Before we do, I want you to take a look inside your own head at what stories you've been telling yourself about selling. After all, you can't change a habit that you don't realize you have. Raising your awareness around the beliefs you've been carrying around about sales will help you re-engineer your thought process.

Exercise: Uncover Your Hidden Beliefs about Selling

Before we get too far into rethinking how you see sales, I want you to take a moment to capture the preconceived notions you have about selling. Why? Because selling likely has negative connotations for you, and no matter how convincing I may be in pointing out the positive—even transformational—aspects of it, your subconscious mind will go to great lengths to avoid doing things it judges to be distasteful. So let's see what's floating around in your subconscious about sales, shall we? Clearing out some of that mental clutter will help you decide which thoughts you want to keep and which you want to let go of.

As a reminder, you can find formatted worksheets of all the exercises in this book at www.MeantForMoreGuide.com. On the worksheet, or in your journal or on a blank document on your computer, write down the following questions and your answers:

- When I hear the word "sales," the first thoughts that pop into my head are . . .

  Door to Door / Telesales - Pushy

- One of my earliest memories of someone selling something is . . .

  Working for NDCS - not very ethical selling, lies

- My family's general attitudes about sales and sales-people were...

  Sleazy, not very nice, don't want to speak with them

- If you tell me I have to get in front of people and sell them something, my first thoughts are...

  Oh shit, what if they say no

  and the immediate feeling that comes up is...

  Fear

Now go back and read through your answers. Can you detect a theme or a specific belief or set of beliefs that has made you uncomfortable with the idea of selling?

At the end of this chapter, we'll rewrite some of that mental programming so that you can open your heart and mind to the power of knowing how to make your offer or extend your invitation—in other words, how to sell. I'll ask you some follow-up questions that will help you write a new set of beliefs about sales. Doing this first piece of the exercise now will create some room for those new thoughts to take root!

EVEN GIVING ADVICE IS A FORM OF SELLING

Maybe you've recently lost a lot of weight by changing your diet and your lifestyle. You're out to lunch with your girlfriends, and they are asking you how you did it. So you tell them about the foods you ate and the types of workouts you did. They listen and nod, but in the end they say, "That sounds too hard." Despite how doable you now know it is, and how much you want your friends to feel as good in their bodies as you now do, they don't do anything with the information you share. They stay the same and you feel like you missed an opportunity to help. Have this happen enough times, and you may conclude that it's better not to talk about your successes or offer advice. But that would be a shame—for you, because you deserve to feel good about your achievements and to use them to help others; and for other people, because they won't get the opportunity to experience the transformation that you could help them with.

To be clear, I'm all for sharing best practices with friends in a social setting. But if they aren't engaged in what you're saying and haven't made a decision to really take in the expertise you're offering, you may as well stick to rehashing old memories together or discussing where you got your purse. It's just too painful to share your expertise with people who don't do anything with it over and over again. They walk away from your well-meaning conversation thinking that it's just too much work to make the changes they're longing to make. And you may decide that it's a bad idea to offer your expertise to others because what's the point? It's a spirit-crusher for both of you—especially you.

If you're talking to someone who sincerely wants to make a change in an area that you can help her with, and you aren't making an invitation for her to partake in whatever it is you have to offer, you're giving your gifts away for free. I know this may sound like a noble thing to do, but the problem is that people value what they pay for and pay for what they value.

I know this pain of giving your gifts away for free so well. When I was married, my then-husband used to call me Mrs. Better Way, because when it came to running our lives—whether it was how to load the dishwasher or manage our finances—I always had a better way. He deferred to me, as did many other people in my life when it came to creating powerful structures that worked. (Now I can see that this ability to create and hone systems is one of my most valuable gifts; but at the time, I didn't even know I had that particular gift, much less appreciate it. I thought it was just me being me.)

The problem is, when you are Mr. or Mrs. Better Way in an area where the receiver did not request feedback or help, things can get ugly. To be honest, it's little wonder that this marriage ended in divorce—how much do you enjoy receiving unsolicited advice from someone you love, over and over and over again? It took many years and a lot of pain from giving advice to people who didn't ask for it for me to realize that I couldn't keep trying to shove my ideas down other people's throats. Rather, there needed to be some kind of opening for me to be able to offer my gifts in a way that could make a difference. In my world, sales is about creating that opening and then making an irresistible offer that serves.

REFRAME THE GAME: A NEW DEFINITION OF SALES

From now on, every time you hear the word "selling" or "sales" out loud or in your head, I want you to replace those words in your mind with "making an invitation." Because that's really what sales is all about—inviting people to take advantage of a compelling opportunity in the form of an irresistible offer. It's about empowering someone to walk through the door of what's possible by their own volition. You don't need to convince them or pursue them—you merely invite them.

An invitation is the simple definition of sales. But there are a lot more wonderful ways to view selling. It is also an opportunity for you to:

- **Share your gifts.** I fully believe that every person on the planet has within them the capacity to touch the lives of others, and that to keep that capacity hidden is a disservice both to you and to the world at large. Selling is how you create the opportunity to share those gifts with the people who need them. That's why my life's mission is to inspire people to own their unique value and have the confidence and courage to open up and make irresistible offers to the people they were meant to serve. (If you're hearing a little voice in your head right now saying, "Gifts? What gifts?" we'll talk about how to discover and unwrap your unique gifts in Chapter 4.)

- **Make a difference.** When you share your gifts with people who are ready to make a change, you exercise the power that resides within each of us to make this world a better place. Think of Miss Julie—the kids she teaches are learning how to use their voices, how practicing something you care about helps you get better, and how they can use their individual voices to contribute to a greater whole. Or imagine you want to talk to your partner about improving your relationship: When you learn how to propose that in an irresistible way, you stand to strengthen your relationship, which will provide a better foundation for each of you to go out and make a difference in this world, as well as a powerful model of a successful relationship for your kids, friends, and family to be inspired by. In this new definition of sales, everyone wins. There are no losers. Imagine if everyone on the planet were focused on using their gifts to create a good outcome for everyone (including themselves). If you do it, it'll be much more likely that others will do it too.

- **Make more money.** It is very true that learning how to get more people to say yes to your irresistible offer can positively impact your bottom line. After all, knowing how to sell means that you'll have more sales! But even if you aren't an entrepreneur, using the Meant for More Formula to name, claim, and value your gifts will help you be a better advocate and negotiator for yourself. You'll see what you are uniquely suited to do—what no one else can do quite like you can—and you'll seek opportunities where the value you bring to the table is needed and rewarded. It is a completely just and natural consequence that putting more value out into the world causes more value to come back to you—and a common form for that value to take is dollar bills (or whatever currency your country uses).

- **Give people an opportunity to say yes to themselves.** In this new definition of selling, you are not seeking to get people to say yes to *you*. You are seeking to get them to say yes to themselves and to commit to taking action that brings them closer to something they want. In other words, you are not the pursuer. The person you're making an offer to is the pursuer. And they aren't pursuing you, they are pursuing their own version of "more." This is comforting news for anyone who thinks that selling is somehow egocentric. It's not. Rather, it's about being of service. Knowing this can help you get over yourself and just show up for the people you were meant to serve without worrying about how it makes you look.

- **Empower people to make a decision.** As powerful as creating that opening for transformation is, it's not enough. That door will only stay open for a short time before the person you're hoping to help will either get distracted by their busy life or their inner critic or well-meaning friends and advisors will start chiming in with all kinds of reasons why the transformation isn't feasible. So one of the aims of your irresistible offer is to provide all the information that person needs to be able to make a decision on the spot, before that door closes. And that decision doesn't even need to be a yes. It's just as valuable for them to hear your offer and say no in the moment. Because then they don't have to sleep on it, talk it over with their spouse, or keep it as an open item in their minds. After all, we all have enough open items on our mental to-do lists; having one more only adds to our general sense of overload. The goal of selling in the Meant for More model is merely to get people to make a choice. By giving people everything they need to be able to make decisions for themselves, you get to sit back and trust that exactly the right people will accept your offer. It removes any subconscious fear of being pushy or manipulative, and that's a beautiful thing.

DON'T FORGET THE PENS!

Little things make a big difference in how many people say yes to your irresistible offer. Once you discover how to craft irresistible offers and empower people to say yes to themselves, you can help more and more people—without also exerting more and more effort—by paying attention to what actually gets people to take you up on your offer. It could be the littlest thing.

Once, my husband and I attended an introductory financial workshop where they offered us an opportunity to join a premium study group. We had been meaning to get our money ducks in a row for years, and my husband and I were both ready to invest in joining the group so we could rest easy, knowing we were paying attention to this important part of our lives. The problem? The line to sign up was too long, and there were no pens available for us to fill out our forms on our own. So we decided to go to lunch and sign up afterward. While we were at lunch, the window of possibility that had opened for us during the morning session started to close. We wondered if this was really the right time. If we would actually do the work. We ended up not signing up. And our path to financial freedom took that much longer—all because there were no pens: we didn't have what we needed to say yes on the spot.

If you want to enroll all the people who want the transformation you're offering, you'll need to focus on the percentage of people who say yes to your offer, or what's known as your sales conversion rate. In a business sense, sales conversion is the percentage of prospects that you turn into paying customers, clients, or patients. In my world, sales conversion is taking someone from "I'll think about it" to "Yes, let's do this!" And learning how to get more yeses helps you help more people and create more good in the world, because getting people to say yes to themselves is what gets them into action and gets them to take responsibility for moving toward their version of "more."

For example, if you give a presentation and make your irresistible offer to a room full of 10 prospects and three of them end up paying you for your services, your conversion rate is 30 percent. If seven of them sign up, your conversion rate is 70 percent.

As you increase your conversion rate, you decrease the amount of work you need to do to earn money and to share your gifts, talents, products, and services with the world. Either way, you spent the same amount of time on making your presentation. But in the second instance, you earned more than twice as much money and helped more than twice as many people. It feels great!

This math is just as true in life. If you can motivate your kids to get their breakfast dishes in the sink, backpacks packed, and shoes and coats on after asking them only once, versus asking them nicely three times and then starting to shout, which then causes everyone's moods to plummet before the day even formally begins, you will save both you and your kids valuable time and energy. If you can entice your department head to implement your idea after one presentation instead of several meetings, e-mails, and phone calls, you get to use the time you've saved to actually make meaningful change *and* you get to enjoy that gratified feeling that you're making a difference much sooner. Better conversion improves everyone's lives. And you'll learn how to do it in Step Four of this book (no smarmy sales techniques required).

WHAT KNOWING HOW TO SELL CREATES FOR YOU

In all, when you learn how to make irresistible offers, you reap the following benefits:

- **No more pursuit.** You no longer have to feel like you have to convince anyone to buy what you're selling, whether that's products, services, ideas, expertise, or advice. You paint a picture of what's possible, give people what they need to make a decision, and trust that the right people will take you up on your offer. And when you learn how to make your offer irresistible, people actually start pursuing *you*. How's that for powerful?

- **No more wishing and waiting.** Knowing how to open up and make an offer means you become the agent of your own success. You don't have to stay frustrated, waiting to be noticed and wondering why you're such a well-kept secret or aren't more successful. When you get comfortable with making offers and putting yourself out there, you create your own opportunities and draw more and better results to you.

- **Doing well by being yourself.** With the structures that you'll learn in Step Four of this book, you gain access to tools that do the selling for you. You don't have to shift into a different gear or be anybody other than your true, authentic self. Knowing how to sell isn't a personality trait, it's a skill. So learn the skills and keep your personality intact.

- **Knowing that you're truly helping others.** When you know how to help people make a decision, you help end the pain that comes from not having clarity about what they want. You empower people to say yes to transformation and give them an opportunity to take ownership of their desires and get into action.

- **Enjoying greater fulfillment.** Using your God-given gifts not only helps others—it helps fulfill your longing for more. You step out of living a "woulda, coulda, shoulda" kind of life, and get to rest in the knowledge that you're doing your part to make the world a better place.

- **Inviting more rewards into your life and the lives of others.** When you share the wealth—in terms of your knowledge, expertise, insight, and gifts—you receive the wealth, which you can then spread around to others in whatever way you see fit. More on this in the very next chapter!

Exercise: Write a New Story about Selling

Now that you've learned about all the wonderful things that knowing how to sell without being sales-y makes possible, let's lay down some new beliefs and make a new commitment to embracing a selling-as-service mentality.

Refer back to your worksheet (which you can download at www.MeantForMoreGuide.com) or the notebook or journal you used for the first exercise in this chapter, and write down the following questions and your answers:

- The new definition of sales that I'm choosing to take on is . . .

  Helping people get closer to their definition of more.

- I now see that learning how to sell makes the following desirable things possible for me . . .

  Sharing my gifts, creating wealth, helping others achieve more

- I hereby commit to viewing sales more positively and will actively seek out opportunities to make more invitations to people I know I can help. (Sign your name below.)

  Signature: *[signature]*

  Date: *9/8/22*

I hope that I have cracked open some new possibilities in your mind regarding what putting your ideas and gifts forward can do for you and the people you're here to help. But I'd understand if you still had some reservations about reaching for your version of more. That's why the next chapter is all about dissipating any remaining doubts or fears and empowering yourself to make more of a difference in a way that feels great both to you and the people you are here to serve.

CHAPTER 2

THE FIRST PERSON YOU NEED TO SELL IS YOURSELF

In Chapter 1, we talked about how selling is actually a service to the person you're making your offer to—how it's really about opening up a door of possibility in their mind and then inviting them to walk through that door toward something they want. It's empowering, even exhilarating, to learn how to make irresistible offers and to help others make meaningful change in their lives. It can also be scary to put yourself out there.

You may read the information in this book and be relieved to discover the very tools you've been missing. You'll be able to make irresistible offers right away and just refine as you go. But it's more likely that, as excited as you may be at the prospect of knowing how to sell, you'll need a little more convincing before you really go for it. That's what this chapter is about—selling yourself on the idea of selling.

IT'S TIME TO THINK BIG

In order to open up the door of possibility for yourself, you've got to give some thought to what you want to invite into your life. Because if you aren't 100 percent clear on why you want to reach for more, you may read to the end of this book, then quickly get pulled back into your busy life and not implement any of the structures I outline here. Which, hey, would be understandable, as we all have plenty on our plates already! It would also mean that you would be that much less likely to make the difference that you were put on this earth to make, or that you would feel depleted by any efforts you do make because you won't be motivated to get over any initial discomfort. You may even tell yourself that learning how to make irresistible offers is too hard, try to shut down that longing for more, and go back to being frustrated. And that's not why you picked up this book—some part of you knows that there is more available to you. So let's turn that vague feeling into a clear vision of the results and rewards you are secretly (or not-so-secretly) craving.

As we go through this chapter that explores the rewards that can come from learning how to sell yourself and your ideas, I want to encourage you to think big—bigger than you may feel you have any right to think. Why? Because sometimes it's hard to connect with what's possible if you haven't experienced it. And even though you're trying to set big goals for yourself, it's easy to set your sights too low.

When I was in college, studying marketing and sales, I aspired to find a 9 to 5 job that paid my bills—at that point in my life, that was the biggest dream I could picture for myself. Shortly after graduating, however, I met someone who helped me upgrade my vision. While attending a tradeshow, I met a man— whom I later started dating—who was a district sales manager for Xerox. He could fly wherever he needed to be to visit vendors throughout the country. When he traveled, he had a budget that covered stays in nice hotels, meals in high-quality restaurants, and tickets to concerts and sporting events. When he wasn't traveling, he could work from home. He also had a budget for training and development, which was *very* appealing to me (I have always been a fan of classes and seminars). When I saw what was possible—the freedom and the first-class lifestyle—I knew I wanted it too. And within six months, I had that same job at a different company. That never would have happened so quickly if I hadn't been inspired by his example.

As you go through this process of naming what you want, it's important to make sure that you're looking for clues in the right places.

ASK YOUR HEART, NOT YOUR HEAD

As important as it is to find examples of other people who are modeling a reality that you want for yourself, you also need to look within yourself. There are two places you can turn to find this inner guidance—your heart or your head. There's only one place that will give you answers that are true for you and not merely ideas of things that you think you should want. That place is your heart—*not* your head.

As much as we prize rational thinking, and as much as your intelligence can help you process new information, your head doesn't always have the most empowering view of things. It's the part of you that's likely to chime in with things like, "Sure, that sounds great, but the last time you said yes to something you didn't follow through; what makes you think you'll go for it this time?" Or "That might work for other people, but not for you." Your head is also the source of all excuses. It will try to convince you that you don't have the time to pursue what you truly want or that you can't afford to take energy away from your kids, your relationship, or your everyday pursuits. These excuses may seem very logical, yet the truth is they are merely a trick of your mind to get you to keep playing small—to stay inside your comfort zone and avoid a chance to grow.

Your heart, on the other hand, always knows what's the next right step and can clearly envision what's possible. When you consider something that you want, you may feel your heart leaping or racing in your chest—a sure sign that you're on to something that leads to your Meant for More. Of course, you may still feel some fear or anxiety coming in, but that's a natural part of taking advantage of opportunity. In general, it's your heart that "knows" what's true for you.

Here's another way to think about it: There's a classic children's book by Lou Austin called *The Little Me and the Great Me*. I read it with my own kids, and recommend it for people of all ages. In it, Austin asserts that we all have a Great Me and a Little Me. The Great Me is the version of yourself that you want to consult when you're making higher choices because it also has your best interests in mind and your highest good in sight. The Great Me is your heart. The Little Me, on the other hand, is often scared and dedicated to keeping you protected. The Little Me, aka your head, is very risk averse.

When it comes to figuring out what you want, you've got to ask the Great Me, because it will lead you to opportunities that provide great results and great rewards. The Little Me will guide you toward goals that are small and that keep you small.

When you consult your heart, you can trust the answers it gives. I'll walk you through my favorite way to do just that at the end of this chapter. First I want to give you some examples of the rewards that acting on your "more" can bring.

THE POWER OF NAMING YOUR DESIRES

In my work with thousands of entrepreneurs over the years, the three most overwhelming reasons *why* people want to discover and deliver their unique gifts to the world are: 1) They are seeking more money. 2) They are seeking more freedom. 3) They want to make more of a difference in the world. Some people have a clear favorite, and some long for all three. Whichever camp you're in, it's helpful to consider each of these areas—because the more clarity you have on what you're seeking to create and why you want it, the more likely you will be to implement all the advice in this book and start making your offers. It never fails to amaze me how naming your desires can propel you to do things differently.

Whatever you do, don't skip over any of the following sections! Because whatever you set your sights on is what you're likely to attract; it would be a shame to tell yourself now that you're not interested in making more money because you're more interested in helping people, when in actuality having more money would help you help more people. Now's the time to entertain all possibilities, then let your heart guide you toward what you truly want.

More Money

I know money is a loaded topic. You may have grown up with the idea that wanting more money is tacky or shallow. Or that people who have money are mean or selfish. Or that if you have a lot of money, then somebody else has less. There are many ways the inner critic will try to convince you that it's not okay to want more money.

If any part of you is cringing about openly admitting that you'd like more money, I want to share my perspective. I firmly believe that money is like water—it will flow wherever there are no impediments to it and that flow will be more plentiful wherever there is momentum. When you are seeking to help other people and making offers that inspire people to invest in that help, you will remove many of your internal blocks to greater success. And when you implement the structures that I'll teach in Step Four of this book, it will be so simple for you to continue to make your offer that you will create momentum in spades.

Whether you picked up this book because you want a bigger income or you just want to get more confident in putting yourself "out there," by implementing the systems in this book, you almost can't help invite more money and abundance into your life. You may decide to build a business out of your gifts, as I did and so many of my clients have. Or you may use these systems to become a better fundraiser. Or a more successful negotiator. Or to get more of what you want out of life more often. And any of these things can lead to more money coming to you and flowing through you.

Because it's difficult to get to a destination if you don't know the address, it's important to get clear on how much more money you'd like to have come your way and what you'd like to do with it when it does. Having this specific vision will motivate you to open up and make your offer.

For me, I was the primary breadwinner of our family when my then-husband was in medical school and my two kids were toddlers. I was working as a one-on-one coach, teaching mission-driven entrepreneurs how to implement the sales systems that I include in this book. I was maxed out, working as many hours as I had available, and my income had topped out at just about six figures. That's a nice amount of money to make, but with daycare expenses and how stretched I was, it always felt like we were one flat tire or chipped tooth away from everything falling apart. That's when I invested in a training program that taught me how to use the internet to attract clients and deliver training and coaching to multiple people at the same time. With that education, my business started doubling. In one ten-month period I went from earning low six figures as a one-on-one coach to making $2.2 million through selling online courses, leading live events, and providing high-level group coaching. The next year it was $4.4 million. Those numbers have continued to increase exponentially.

Perhaps the idea of millions of dollars seems too far-fetched. If that's the case, Doreen's story might be more inspiring: A devoted educator, Doreen has been an academic college counselor for an all-boys high school for nearly three decades. Doreen works with students from the ninth grade all the way through their graduation at the end of senior year. For the younger boys, she mostly advises on things like time management and making sure they take a well-rounded course load. Once her students become juniors, she guides them through the college application process—an emotionally loaded challenge as well as a huge logistical project that requires a lot of time on top of the regular load of homework. Although Doreen loves helping her students find the right college, there was only so much individualized attention she could give to each student in the midst of her regular workday catering to a full student body.

In response to requests from parents whose children don't attend that school for guidance, Doreen developed a two-hour seminar that was free to attend and held it in her living room. Twelve moms attended. In those two hours, Doreen gave them as much information and answered as many questions as she could. Then she followed the selling structures I outline in Step Four of this book and made an offer to the women to join a six-week seminar priced at $1,000 that went way beyond the basics and provided everything Doreen knew about getting into college as well as plenty of time for personal attention. Every single one of the women said yes. In that very first seminar, Doreen made $12,000. As someone who'd never remotely considered herself a salesperson, Doreen was floored. As she's said, "I'm a college counselor; there's no selling in my job. Well, I try to sell advice to kids, and they often don't take it!"

After running that first seminar, Doreen launched College Prep Roadmap—a business that helps kids and families who need college counseling. As she says, "I am proud to serve these families, and do it in such a way that makes the process fun!"

Doreen will tell you she's really not in it for the money—after all, she's still working at the job she loves at the all-boys high school (she runs the business with the school administration's blessing). The primary reason she does it is because she truly loves partnering with families and empowering them to find the right college fit. Yet Doreen will also tell you that she loves the added income. She has used the money she's made from her seminars to contribute to her family, funding "nice-to-haves" like home renovation projects and vacations.

My story and Doreen's story are great examples of this basic principle:

> *When you share the wealth (whether it's your time, energy, or expertise), it makes sense that you ought to receive wealth in return.*

More Freedom

When you get clear on the value you can deliver to others and start making offers to deliver that value in a way that gets people to say yes to themselves, something magical happens: You free yourself from having to do all the other hundreds of little things that don't require your unique genius to accomplish. This releases you from that feeling that I hear so many people complaining about—feeling shackled by their to-do lists, having too many balls in the air, and never having enough time to get everything done.

Tammy Foley, a graduate of my training programs, exemplifies this freedom perfectly. Tammy was a single mom who ran a bookkeeping business for 28 years, and a successful business at that—Tammy did so well that she could afford to send her children to private school even though she was the sole parent and earner in the family. Although Tammy was great at the actual bookkeeping, what she really loved doing was teaching others to get their financial ducks in a row.

When Tammy and I first met, she had already developed an online training course where she taught entrepreneurs everything they needed to know to make more money and keep more of it for themselves. In order to complete the course, Tammy had already started delegating some of the day-to-day operations of her bookkeeping business to her staff. To her surprise and delight, Tammy realized that her staff was more than capable of taking on more responsibility, which then freed her up to focus even more time and energy on selling and improving her course. Things were moving along well for Tammy. Then tragedy struck.

Tammy's grandniece was killed in a horrific accident. Tammy's nephew was distraught, as were his other six children. Tammy didn't skip a beat—she picked up and went to stay with her nephew for 10 days, entrusting the business to her staff in her absence. She recalls that she didn't get one phone call or e-mail about work while she was gone—her learning how to delegate and empowering other people to do the job without micromanaging meant the business didn't miss a beat without her.

Once she returned to work, even as she moved through her mourning period, Tammy was inspired to take even more off her plate and get out there in a bigger way, selling her courses to entrepreneurs who were seeking greater prosperity by doing what made their hearts sing. And so she handed over even more responsibility to her staff and poured herself into developing, selling, and leading those courses, which fueled even more growth in her revenue and her business.

Tammy isn't the only one who benefits here. Her staff gets the chance to feel worthy of trust and to grow their skills, responsibilities, and income levels. Tammy's clients also get better service that isn't dependent on any one person's availability. And the hundreds of people who take Tammy's courses get the benefit of learning how to better manage their own finances so that they too have the freedom to pursue the things they love the most instead of constantly feeling like they have to be working to keep their coffers filled.

The greater point of Tammy's story is this: Just because you can do something well doesn't mean you have to be the one to do it—particularly if it keeps you from helping others in a bigger way! In Tammy's case, creating and delivering those courses allowed her to help more business owners than she could have if her company did all the work for them. It also enabled her to have a lifestyle in which she could be there for her family when they needed support at a crucial time. Think about what you would do if you were free from the menial tasks that eat up so much of your time—would you travel, pursue a creative project, start the side hustle you've been dreaming about, or spend more time with family? Whatever you're longing for, learning how to sell will help make that possible for you.

More of a Difference

For many people, that feeling that you were meant for more is a strong hunch that you are capable of doing more good in the world. More money would be nice, sure, but at the end of the day, what's driving you is a sincere desire to make a difference.

One of the members of my online training community, Kathy Marks, is a great example of this. Kathy was in corporate sales. She regularly generated $5 million for the corporation she worked for and was compensated $300,000 for her efforts. It was definitely a nice salary, but the mission of the company didn't really move her, and Kathy felt that if she started her own business, even if she generated less than the $5 million she knew she was capable of creating, she'd reap more of the rewards and have more freedom. What truly motivated Kathy was a desire to put her energy into something that would help others. So she took a leap.

Kathy opened a consulting practice for independent physicians, who often struggle to make enough money to keep the doors open in the changing medical landscape. As she says, "Most doctors are in medicine to serve; it's a calling for them. They take care of our most important assets—our health and the health of our families. It's so fulfilling to open up new worlds for health-care providers by following my own purpose." In addition to helping doctors continue to serve their patients and create good lives for themselves and their families, Kathy has also created a multiple-six-figure business for herself—proof that even when your primary motivator is giving back, you can still do well for yourself.

And it's not just the doctors who work with Kathy directly who benefit—it's also their employees and their hundreds of patients. When you think of all the lives that Kathy has an effect on through her work, you can start to see just how much power one person has to help countless others. If your "meant for more" helps others help others—if you are a body worker, mental health counselor, or business coach, for example—the benefit of your efforts is exponential.

Exercise: Name What You Want, Why You Want It, and How It Will Help Others

As powerful as it is to seek answers from your heart, it's not necessarily easy. The head will likely try to butt in and run the show. That's why I love the method that I'm about to share with you. It essentially gives the voice that comes from your heart a microphone—or more accurately, a pen.

I learned about this method in Tim Kelly's wonderful book *True Purpose*. Kelly says that the exercise he calls "Active Imagination" originated with Carl Jung, one of the fathers of modern psychology.

I've also heard what I'm about to share called "automatic writing." No matter what you call it, it's a process of consulting your heart that's simple yet very powerful. You can do it through meditation or prayer, although I suggest that you get out your journal again and write down your questions and answers. (You can also find this exercise in worksheet form at www.MeantForMoreGuide.com.) Whichever method you choose, all you need to do is ask questions and then listen for—and accept without judgment—the answers you hear.

The process that works for me and, according to Tim's book, works for about 75 percent of people who try it, is a two-way written dialogue between you and your heart, which is really a conduit for the divine, God, or the universe—whatever you like to call it. Tim refers to this entity as your "Trusted Source," so that's what I'll use here. It's a lot like the book *Conversations with God*, in which Neale Donald Walsh reveals his back-and-forth conversation with God.

Even though I had never tried anything like this before, I managed to access my Trusted Source, and got great answers.

My conversation went something like this:

Lisa: Hello, God, are you available for a chat?

God: Yes, I've been waiting for you to show up and talk to me here.

Lisa: Wow! This is a lot more than I expected.

God: Good. You should expect to get a lot more than you expected when you talk with me.

Just as Tim coached me to do, I asked questions and started getting answers on several things—general inquiries as well as specific questions on business strategy, my love life, how to interact with my children, and much more. Of course my Little Me wondered if it was just me writing back and forth to myself. In his book, Tim assures us, "That's a healthy human psyche resisting change."

The more I did this process and took action on the guidance I was getting, the more I knew these conversations were very real. My Trusted Source would commonly use words that I would never have chosen. Many times this gave me the chills as the pen revealed the next insight. In many other instances, my Trusted Source was actually funny. Apparently, that's another sign that you are truly connecting. I've had the privilege to have Tim on my stage as a guest sharing this technique with many of my students, and I've seen firsthand how powerful it can be if you use the Active Imagination writing process to uncover what's on your heart.

Try your own Active Imagination session to ask your Trusted Source to reveal the desires of your heart. It will help expand your idea of what's available to you and put a fire in your belly to pursue it.

First, give your Trusted Source a name, whether you want to call it God, Life, Spirit, or something else. Then write out a conversation as if you were writing a play. Just as I did in the example I shared above, write down your name and a colon followed by your question. Then write your Trusted Source's name and a colon and capture whatever answer you hear in writing. Remember, you want this to be a dialogue, not a one-way conversation. So be sure to give each party—you and your Trusted Source—a chance to speak for itself.

The tricky thing is I can't tell you exactly what to write or even what to ask. I can only give you these starting prompts:

- You: Hello there, (insert your Trusted Source's name). Are you available for a chat?

- You: I'd like to get your opinion on what you think my unique gifts are.

- You: How do you think I might make the biggest difference in the world using my gifts?

- You: What do you think using my gifts will make possible in my life, the lives of the people I love, and the people I help?

- You: What other possibilities can you see that perhaps I can't see yet?

I think you'll be pleasantly surprised by the depth and detail of the answers you receive. And if you think you're one of the 25 percent of people who don't get valuable information from the Active Imagination exercise, you can ask these same questions of a couple of people you absolutely trust to see the best in you. A little objectivity can go a very long way toward bringing new possibilities into view!

KEEPING THE DOOR OF POSSIBILITY OPEN

Getting clear on what you uniquely offer and gearing up to make your irresistible offer is going to create a lot of new possibilities in your mind, which is great. The problem is that possibility is like a door—it can lead you to wonderful new places, but it doesn't stay open forever. I'm guessing you've had a flash of insight before—where you can see exactly how you can make some important change. Sometimes you can sense exactly how that change is going to make you feel even though you haven't yet done anything to make it real. It's an exciting space to be in. But if you don't take some action to make that possibility real, the door that opened for you in a flash will just as quickly swing shut. You'll go back into your normal life and get distracted by your inbox or what to have for dinner, and before you know it, you've forgotten all about that new possibility.

Possibility is like a vivid dream that seems so real the moment you wake up. You're so excited about this dream and you want to tell your honey all about it, but you decide to run to the bathroom real quick first. By the time you get back into bed, it's gone and you're left with only a vague idea of what it was about, or perhaps you've forgotten it altogether.

Like the wooden wedges you see holding big doors open, you too need a tangible structure to shove into the doorway to keep that open door of possibility from slamming shut. That's why people create vision boards and form-reading groups or invest in courses and group programs like the ones I offer.

These kinds of structures keep you present to what you are trying to create. They can also help you surround yourself with people who can see exciting possibilities for themselves and who are committed to taking action toward them. Immersing yourself in a community of like-minded people is so important, because talking about how to reach for your version of more isn't a typical topic of conversation in most households or friendship circles. If you start talking about and hanging up pictures of your "why" and then start taking action toward it, some people may tell you you're crazy. I am here to tell you that *you're not the only one.* There are plenty of people out there who feel that they too are meant for more and who are working on making that "more" come true.

If you're struggling to find the willingness to start making your offers, put yourself in places—either live or virtual—where you can surround yourself with other people who share your sense of possibility. Just as importantly, minimize the time you spend around people who sound a lot like your Little Me. Suggest to like-minded friends that you start a regular accountability group. Find a real-world networking group or Facebook tribe of people who are seeking to create new opportunities for themselves. Join me at LisaSasevichFan.com so you can connect with our awesome tribe on Facebook. You may want to invest in a coaching program that can give you guidance and a community of people dedicated to reaching for more.

Staying in touch with your own desires can prompt you to keep making your offer, even when your Little Me would really rather you didn't, or tries to convince you that you're too tired, too introverted, or too *something* to put yourself out there.

I know that it may feel uncomfortable to do something you've been resistant to. That resistance may seem like a sign to stop—it's not. As Tim Kelly said, resistance is merely a sign of a healthy human psyche resisting change. And change is what you're after. To help you get going and keep going whenever resistance hits, it helps to reinterpret that uncomfortable feeling as stretching. If it's a sign of anything, it signifies that you are heading in the right direction, toward whatever "more" looks like to you. Breathe into it, and rest when you need to, but keep coming back to it. Keep tapping into your willingness to change. That's how you grow.

CHAPTER 3

LIFT AS YOU CLIMB

I hope you are starting to get on board with the idea of selling yourself, your ideas, and your expertise so that you can do more good and receive more rewards. Now I want to show you that the benefits of accepting that you are meant for more don't stop there. You have the capacity within you to touch the lives of others—you just have to be willing to make your irresistible offer.

I know that for women especially it can be difficult to get comfortable with the idea of selling yourself simply because you picked up along the way that it's nicer and more ladylike to wait to be noticed. Or perhaps you got the message that it's safer not to stand out. Or that it's a smart strategy to keep your desires small so that you don't get disappointed. Or that if you really cared and truly had the desire to help people, you'd do it for free. So many of us internalized these messages growing up. Their popularity doesn't make them true.

I also know that because many women are natural-born caretakers, when they start to realize that sharing their gifts and making their offers can help others, they can get motivated, fast. I've seen it happen time and time again—when women realize how much power they have to help others, they find the desire and confidence to start selling their advice, expertise, gifts, and talents in a bigger way.

LOOK FOR THE WIN-WIN

The simple truth is that selling your help via your gifts, talents, services, knowledge, and expertise is about so much more than you; it's about creating the highest good for *everyone*, including you.

I'm not naïve. I know that the Meant for More Formula can be used with good or not-so-good intent; if you just want to make a buck with the strategies within it, you can. Yet I have found that the people who truly understand the tools I teach—and who have the most success with them—are committed to being agents of change. Even though we are regular people, we are willing to step up as leaders and share the path we've stumbled on to. And when we make money from sharing that path, we also commit to expanding our giving and increasing our ability to make a difference even more by supporting the people and organizations that are furthering the causes we care about.

In many cases, the advice, coaching, or expertise you're offering came to you as the result of a struggle you've overcome or a time when you've beat the odds. Whatever it is—perhaps you grew up poor yet you learned how to save and put yourself through college, and now you want to help other people do the same—it probably seemed insurmountable initially. You may think that you can't possibly help people do what you did. That was the case for me—I didn't think I could possibly teach anyone else how to make an irresistible offer because it was something I had always done without much awareness of *how* I was doing it. I felt so awkward at first, inviting people to learn how to make their offer! But once I realized that making my offer was helping people get out there with their offer and make the difference that they were put here to make, I got over that fear fast. The reality is, whatever your definition of more is, if you are offering it from your heart, it can open new possibilities for other people that they may not be able to initiate on their own. It gives them the chance to move out of a victim role, in which there is little hope or inspiration to change, to taking charge of their lives so that they can grow.

Personally, I believe it is a disservice not to make an offer to someone who can benefit from your unique gifts. In fact, the offer is more for them than for you. It allows them the chance to really see, in a black-and-white way, if they are serious about growing. For example, if one of your friends confides in you that she wants to take better care of her diabetes, and you're an expert in this area because you've changed your diet and gotten off your meds, what happens if you wave her off because you aren't confident in your ability to help? Or what happens if you agree to meet her for coffee so she can pick your brain; she asks you a million questions and you tell her everything you can, but you don't make an irresistible offer? I'll tell you what happens: She will probably do nothing about her health, and you will feel taken advantage of and perhaps even walk away thinking that it's better not to talk to other people about how you healed your diabetes. Then you'll start doubting the power of what you truly know and won't make an offer to help the next person who comes along, even though that person may be dreaming of doing exactly what you've done to gain control of your health.

Because of this power that you have to affect others:

> *It's a gift to make your offer to a person you can help.*

If you make an offer to someone and she accepts it, it's a beautiful thing. You've gotten a person to step up to the table who now has a strong likelihood of taking action that will move her closer to her dreams.

If she says no, there is still a gift in your having made your offer. You've given her the opportunity to see where she truly stands. A time for her to look at herself in the mirror, maybe for the first time. A chance to take personal responsibility for something that's been bothering her, maybe for the first time ever. She may not be ready to take action right now, and that's okay. At least now she knows she's not ready and can stop beating herself up for not making progress. It's an honesty process. And that level of clarity is ultimately in service of her highest good, because indecision and ambiguity are surefire ways to stay stuck.

Whenever you hesitate before making an offer, just remember that it's a service to make your offer, and to make it irresistible. Indeed, Jay Abraham, a well-known sales expert, says it's your moral obligation to make an offer—that's how beneficial to others it is.

ONE WOMAN'S POWER TO CHANGE MANY LIVES

One of the women I have mentored, Kerry Ann Rockquemore, was a sociology professor for 12 years. Although Kerry Ann had lifelong job security because she had earned tenure as a professor, she felt that the six-year process of getting tenure was one of the most difficult periods of her life. With no one to mentor her through the process of conducting research, publishing papers, and doing service projects, Kerry Ann had made one mistake after another during her quest for tenure, and had felt horribly embarrassed and exhausted by the whole endeavor to the point that it negatively impacted her job satisfaction. And as a woman of color, Kerry Ann was also dismayed to see that there were so few professors with diverse racial backgrounds.

When Kerry Ann finally earned her tenure, she was so miserable she decided that no one should have to go through the process without a knowledgeable, caring guide. So she wrote a book, *The Black Academic's Guide to Winning Tenure—Without Losing Your Soul*, began working with professors at her university, and spoke at other institutions. Her side business grew to the point that Kerry Ann had to make a choice—either remain a full-time, tenured professor with lifetime job security or devote herself to helping other academic women of color land their own tenured positions. Kerry Ann knew that she loved helping the other professors much more than she enjoyed the research and publishing parts of her professor job. So she decided to make the leap.

A true academic with no business training or background to speak of, Kerry Ann knew she needed mentoring. When she joined my Sales, Authenticity, and Success Business Academy for entrepreneurs, she had a handful of clients and $175,000 in annual revenue. In seven years, she grew her business—which consists of an online community, books, speaking engagements, and online courses—to $6 million a year. And she did it in such a way that she and her husband take a month off every year—the business suits her life instead of the other way around.

What's even more important to Kerry Ann than the bottom line is that that business now serves over 82,000 professors at over 450 colleges and universities. Each one of those professors is thriving—publishing new papers regularly, having a life outside of work, and being present for their students. And as impressive as these numbers are, the impact of Kerry Ann's work doesn't stop there. Think about it: Each of those professors teaches hundreds of students a year. And they have the bandwidth to truly be present with their students and serve as advisors, mentors, and role models. Even the students who don't take classes with these professors see them on campus and have their minds opened to what a successful academic looks like: healthy, rested, happy, prolific, and in many cases, female, black and/or another ethnicity besides Caucasian. Kerry Ann's work literally benefits thousands of people *each year.* This is the kind of impact you can have when you follow that voice and lead with your gifts and deliver your unique value. And, as Kerry Ann points out, she does it all while working less than she did as a professor.

Exercise: Calculate Your Ripple

As I said at the beginning of this chapter, women tend to get over their reservations about making offers really quickly when they realize just how many people they can positively impact by offering their gifts. This exercise is designed to help you see the extent of the benefits that you are capable of creating.

Grab your notebook or journal and answer the following prompts, or refer to the companion worksheet that's available at www.MeantForMoreGuide.com.

- Think about someone you've helped in the past. It could be a client, a friend, or a stranger on the street. It could even be you, if there's some big challenge that you've overcome in your life. What changed for them when you offered your help? Really drill down. Did they get a promotion, make more money, lose weight, improve their health, have fewer fights with their spouse, or stop procrastinating?

- What intangible benefits did they receive—an important insight, more self-confidence, an improved relationship, lowered stress, more fun?

- What might have happened if this person hadn't had your help? You'll probably have to do some educated guessing here, but give it a shot. Would this person's stress still be high? Would she have never met her boyfriend? Later on, if you decide to start offering your gifts as a product or service that you are paid for, the answer to this question in particular will help determine a monetary value of what you're offering, so don't skip this step.

- Finally, think about all the people who come into contact with the person you helped—their spouses, kids, family members, coworkers, and clients—and list all the ways those people benefitted from the changes you helped create.

Whenever you feel hesitant, shy, or resistant about making your offer, think of all these ripples that won't happen if you don't try, and let that motivate you!

The world needs what only you have to give. How long do you want to keep hiding it from others? From yourself? How many people will you allow to stay stuck because they don't have access to that magic touch only you have?

STOP LETTING PEOPLE PICK YOUR BRAIN

How many times has someone asked to pick your brain about something you either know a lot about or have a lot of experience with? It's an honor to be recognized as an expert in a particular area. And you want to be nice. So you probably say yes. You find two hours in your schedule to meet for coffee with the intention of being helpful and a vague hope that the person you're meeting with may actually do something with what you share.

When the two of you are at the coffee shop, because of your concerns about being pushy or assumptive, you don't say, "Would you like to work on this together?" And even though you had such a good intention to be helpful, you get that hollow feeling when you're walking out to your car that you somehow missed a chance to make an impact. What happened?

Here's the thing: Letting someone pick your brain without making an offer to help the person who's doing the picking is like rowing the person out into the lake of possibility and leaving her there with no oars. You have a way to help but don't give her the chance to step up and make a commitment to doing something about it. And then boom, that possibility is gone.

When you spend time with someone and give away your gifts for free, without inviting them to learn your system and enjoy the transformation that only you can provide, you walk away with the false assumption that they'll take action with what you shared. The truth is, they won't. Their greatest moment of inspiration is when they're with you—that's when the door of possibility is open to its widest point. They don't walk away and get more inspired. They start to get pulled back into their busy lives, and the door of possibility that seemed so real when they were talking with you starts to swing shut.

As generous as it is to want to help people, at some point it becomes a soul-crusher to give your gifts away without getting anything in return, including the satisfaction of your advice actually helping the receiver. You see, it's okay to share some specific advice to get people started and have them see the power of your gift, but if you give your gold away over the long term, it can hurt you and it can weaken your gift if it's continually not acted upon.

A common result of giving your gifts away for free and having people do nothing with the information you've shared over and over and over again is a profound sense of disempowerment. If that happens, you're likely to tuck your gifts away, sometimes never to be pulled out of the vault again. It was too painful the last time you tried to help. Then all the people you could help don't get the benefit of your attention and expertise. And all the people they come into contact with don't get to experience the ripple effects of their transformation. At the end of the day, it hurts everyone.

Remember, possibility is a door that only stays open for a short time. You want to give the people you can help something to say yes to in that moment—some structure of either a meeting, a class, some coaching, a training video, or an initial service that keeps the possibility open and nudges them to make a decision and either say, "Yes, I'm ready," or "No, I'm not ready." Because transformation only comes after a person has made a decision to do something differently. And if you don't make an offer, you don't give the person you're talking to the chance to decide whether or not they truly want to transform.

Another downside to letting people pick your brain and not making an offer is that you end up doing the heavy lifting for your competition. You're opening the possibilities and someone else is coming in and getting the business. Oof, I know this hurts to hear—please don't shoot the messenger! The truth is, if you can't walk the people you can help through that open possibility, someone else will do it. And because you spent so much time and energy on helping them get present to their pain and to possibility, the next person's job will be that much easier.

A lot of times people believe that if you're good at something or it comes to you naturally, that it should be given freely—it's a gift from God, and so you should gift it to other people. While that may be true in some cases, the challenge is that when people pay for something, they pay attention. Remember, people pay for what they value and value what they pay for.

When someone shows up to see you, chats with you at a networking event or party, or asks you a question about something you know a lot about, they are sending you a message. And what they are saying by giving you their attention is, "I have pain in the area of your expertise," or "That's an area where I'd like to be even better." There's some dissatisfaction there. There's a gap between where they are and where they want to be. Even if things are pretty good with them, they have a longing for more. Otherwise, why would they be asking all those questions? There are so many other things they could be sharing with you or doing with their time and attention.

If after sharing generously and socially, you don't tell them, "Here's how I could help you even further in this area," you're leaving them hanging. If you would just make your offer, they can go straight to getting support instead of constantly talking about what they need without ever actually getting it.

If you really want to share your knowledge with no expectation of anything in return, write down the most important takeaways about the subject you're an expert in and put it in a nice-looking PDF. That way, when someone asks if they can pick your brain, you can say, "Good news! I've already picked it for you!" Then you get to share the information without having to take the time to do it one-on-one over and over and over again. If the person has specific questions for you after reading your brain pickings, you can have a quicker conversation about it. You can still make your offer to work on it further together in that shorter call. Either way, you will have saved yourself a lot of time and energy by passing along the bulk of the information.

The other great thing about this plan is that it puts the onus of action on them. You'll be amazed at how many times they don't even read the PDF. You will have saved yourself yet another coffee shop "pick-your-brain" date that turns out to be informational but not transformational.

BE A RIVER, NOT A POND

As I mentioned in Chapter 2, money is like water—it flows wherever there are no impediments. Just as it is right for you to receive money in return for sharing your unique gift and creating positive change in the world, it is also right for you to send money back out into the world where it can do more good.

We'll cover this more in Step Five, but it's so important that I want you to start wrapping your brain around it now. When you give to others, you become more like a river—where good things flow toward you, and you in turn send good things out into the world—than a pond, where you hold on to any rewards that come your way. As a river you are constantly receiving new money as well as sending it downstream. A pond, on the other hand, has no reliable way of replenishment other than whenever it happens to rain and no way to send water back out into the ecosystem. A river is alive and vibrant and can handle a large increase in flow, while a pond is prone to stagnation. Which one do you want to be?

I have found time and time again that the more you give, the more you get back. Since I started practicing tithing in 2008, I've had countless examples of giving freely, with no expectation or desire for anything in return, and then, to my surprise, receiving the most incredible blessings in my life that come from the most unexpected people and places.

Some years ago I decided to incorporate a fundraising component at each of the live events I host—I really relish the opportunity to support people and organizations that inspire me. I found that offering my participants a chance to contribute while they were learning had some magical unexpected effects. First, it bonded our community in a way that was beyond anything I'd imagined. There's something about giving together that created a bigger space of possibility than we had ever seen before; people were making personal and business connections at a new level. And second, once we started incorporating the giving into our events, miraculously, our participants were able to receive more insight on the spot. Our trainings are so chock-full of mind-expanding information that it's easy to feel like your cup runneth over by the second day, and there's still a full day to go. Once we all started giving, it was as if the giving cleared out some space in the hearts and minds of our participants, and they started having breakthroughs and aha moments more than ever before. It was a counterintuitive surprise; such is the power of giving!

At one of my training events, I raised funds for Global Dental Relief, an organization that my uncle, who was a pediatric dentist, had been doing a lot of work with following his retirement. This group travels all over the world to provide free dental care to kids in need. I'd been dreaming of accompanying my uncle on one of these trips, but my kids were still young and I already traveled a lot for work—I didn't want to be away from them any more than I already was. I got to meet the director of the organization when she came out to San Diego to attend our event. She met my family and ended up inviting me and my son, who was ten at the time, on a trip to Cambodia. I got to take that trip and still be with my son, my son got the experience of traveling and helping others (he led the brushing clinic and administered fluoride treatments), and the organization received a sizable donation from the collective donations of my event attendees. I couldn't have planned it working out that well—it's an example of how things fall into place when you give using the resources you have in a way that feels good and doable to you.

STEP TWO

CLAIM YOUR GIFTS

Have you ever had a moment while doing your work where you thought, "Am I really getting paid for this? It's so easy!" If not, you're in for a big surprise. It is entirely possible that you could be paid the most for doing the thing that is easiest for you to do. That unique skill, knowledge, or expertise that you've either learned or were born with—that other people struggle with—is what I call your million-dollar value.

In Step Two of the Meant for More Formula, you'll do some illuminating work to get crystal clear on your million-dollar value. Then you can ensure your arrow is pointed in the right direction so that when you begin to take action, your action is as effective as it can be. You'll be leading with your best stuff—and the things that come most naturally to you—every step of the way so that you're making the biggest impact possible.

Once you distill that million-dollar value, you'll give it a name by assigning yourself an expert title (in Chapter 5)—an exercise that's like rocket fuel for your clarity and confidence. When you discover your million-dollar value and begin to clarify that "something special" about you that is unique from what anyone else on the planet provides, that's when you start to become unstoppable, and that feeling inside that you were meant for more starts to become real.

CHAPTER 4

DISCOVER YOUR MILLION-DOLLAR VALUE

You, like every single person alive, have a one-of-a-kind set of gifts: talents and skills that come so easily to you or that you enjoy so much that you can't *not* do them. I call them your gifts, your unique value, your million-dollar value, or sometimes your "thing." No matter what you call them, though, these gifts play a big part in making you who you are and empowering you to make the difference you were put here to make.

If you haven't uncovered your unique value yet, that's a major reason why you're feeling like the things you want are out of reach—you haven't been using your most valuable assets. It's like you've been trying to climb a mountain using a toothpick and a dog leash when you've had a pickax and a set of ropes in your backpack all along.

If you aren't fully aware of what those gifts are, you—and the people you are meant to serve—are missing out, because when you are using your gifts, you deliver value like nobody else can, create the biggest impact, and attract the biggest rewards.

It's a fundamental truth that:

> *The best way to make a difference is to use your gifts.*

Yet since you picked up this book (or someone who loves you bought it for you), it's likely that you aren't totally clear on what your one-of-a-kind gifts are. You're in no way alone in this; most people have only a vague idea of what their blessings are because it's not easy to see them for yourself. Why? Because you're so close to it. It's like putting your finger at the tip of your nose and trying to see your fingertip. Try it now! You literally can't see it there because it's just too close for your eyes to be able to register it.

HOW TO UNWRAP YOUR GIFTS

Your gifts can come in many forms. Some are the result of things you've experienced in your life. Others were factory installed—you were born with them. Some of your gifts may lie in your physical design. Think about personal development guru Tony Robbins. He was made to be on stage—at well over six feet tall with huge hands and a booming voice, he is nearly impossible to ignore. His presence is captivating and his energy is invigorating.

Your gifts may be something more psychological—a sensitivity to the feelings of others, for example. Or they could be tangible skills that come easily to you, such as an artistic ability or a facility with numbers.

And then there are your hard-earned talents and expertise that you've developed through your personal and professional experiences. Think of Doreen, whose story I shared in Chapter 2. She was a guidance counselor for nearly three decades before she started coaching families through the college application process—she could do that because she'd developed a deep understanding of how to find the right college, produce a college application that gets results, and support young adults and their families through academic challenges.

48

Maybe you've been a social media maven since these platforms were first released and have a special knack for engaging an audience or building a following, or you've been an office administrator for the last 15 years and every office you work in runs like clockwork, or you've spent much of your spare time reading self-help books and attending personal development seminars, or you've worked hard to have an amicable divorce and a productive co-parenting relationship with your ex. Anything that you've learned at the hands of experience contributes to your gifts.

Your gifts can also be something that you inherited from your family members. I know that some of my blessings come from my Jewish nature of being a little on the aggressive side. I don't trust easily—I need an irresistible offer to get me into action or else I'll research and ask friends and not say yes to things that are calling to me before the door of possibility closes. It's no wonder I teach what I teach about how to make offers irresistible and sell without being sales-y. Have you ever heard the saying "You teach the things you need to learn the most"? Raising my own hand on this one!

As I mentioned in the introduction to this book, my dad was an entertainer. He lived for the stage and he was funny—he was not afraid to say the unsayable, and I got a lot of my ability to speak to people and talk about things like making money and making offers (things that many people shy away from) from him. My mom, on the other hand, was one of those people whom everyone loved. With a big smile and warm heart, she had an "it" factor that I also inherited that makes it easy for me to connect with people I've just met and make them feel as if we've known each other forever. You'll see the roots of your blessings in your family members if you look.

Sometimes your blessings can be wrapped in tough-to-swallow packages—like being fired. When I still worked for other people, I came to see that I was good at making big money for them in really cost-effective and efficient ways, whether they were huge corporations or small personal development companies. Yet I wasn't truly aware of how deep my gift for selling was until I got fired from the company where I thought I'd be working forever. As devastating as being fired was, it was also the wake-up call that started me on my current path.

In truth, while I was working for other people I had often wondered what my "thing" was. I had never searched for an answer because I wasn't forced to find out what it was. Sometimes if you don't take the little taps that the universe gives you, you get the 2 x 4.

Whatever it takes to acknowledge your blessings is perfect. Once you do, you'll see that all the things that add up to your blessings create a package that is completely one of a kind and tailored to help you make the difference that only you can make. Understanding your gifts is a crucial part of figuring out what you have to offer the world and where you can have the biggest impact.

UNCOVER YOUR MILLION-DOLLAR VALUE

Each of us was made for a specific purpose, a transformation that you were uniquely designed to deliver. It's the thing that all your gifts and blessings enable you to do in a way that no one else quite can. This thing is your million-dollar value.

It's called "million-dollar" because these skills, talents, knowledge, and gifts that come so naturally to you that you can't stop doing them even if you tried are what you should be paid the most for. (Take it from me, it's much better to be paid for these talents than to simply be known as a Mr. or Mrs. Better Way.)

I want you to pause and let this sink in for a minute:

> *You can and should be paid the most for the things that come the easiest to you.*

Most people are shocked to learn this, but think about it: We each have unique gifts, right? The emphasis is on the word *unique*.

What is easy, fun, and natural to you is going to be difficult or mysterious for others. Therefore, they should pay you for your unique gifts and vice versa—because the things that are easy, fun, and natural to them might be difficult for you.

In many cases everyone around you can see your million-dollar value better than you can. You can tell they do because they keep coming to you and asking for your advice in this area. During my young adulthood, many people tried to sign me up to be on the sales teams of their network marketing businesses because they could tell that if I were on their team, they'd make a lot of money. They could see that making offers in a way that truly serves came naturally to me, even though I couldn't see it. (Yet.)

After I got fired from my dream job, I was feeling pretty distressed about being back to square one. How was I going to make a difference in my lifetime? I wasn't back at square one, though. Like so many people, I had a million-dollar value that I just couldn't see.

I was shocked by how excited my coach was when I told him I regularly closed such a high percentage of the room on the spot. I didn't even realize how difficult that was for other people to do. That's one of the first steps to identifying your thing. (I'll walk you through the four ways to uncovering your million-dollar value a little later in this chapter, so don't worry—you'll get more detailed instruction soon!) It's generally something you do very easily, almost without a second thought, that other people find hard, mysterious, or even downright distasteful. People will say, "Oh my goodness, how did you *do* that?" Even though it comes naturally to you, it's astonishing to other people and is incredibly valuable to someone who needs what you have to offer.

As I mentioned earlier, it's hard for you to spot your own gifts because you're simply so close to them that they are hard to see. There's also another, deeper reason they often stay hidden: We think that delivering value has to be the result of hard work. Unfortunately, that's why so many naturally talented people don't make the money they're capable of—because they didn't have to struggle to obtain their gifts.

We're so programmed to believe that success has to come from working like a dog that we tend to dismiss things that come easily. If it's that easy to do, this thinking goes, it must not be worth much. Even worse is that we really look down on getting paid to do the things we enjoy. It's like work has to be almost really onerous in order to count. These thoughts are the opposite of the truth, which is that the things that come naturally to you and that you would do whether you were getting paid to do them or not are some of your biggest assets! These things you can't help doing because you've been doing them your whole life are the things you can be paid the most for. They are the tools you can use to deliver the most value and receive the biggest rewards in return.

I do want to be clear—even when you're using your gifts, you will still have work to do; it just won't necessarily feel like work. When you're doing the things you were designed to do, you can go all day. Work energizes you instead of draining you. Also, the things that come the easiest to you can evolve over time. You may be a great office manager, and thus it may make sense for you to start consulting with small businesses on how to set up their processes for maximum productivity. Then, once you start doing that, you may realize you really have a knack for helping business owners develop new revenue streams that they hadn't considered before. In that case, you might still use your organizational skills and head for developing processes and systems, just for a bigger purpose. When you're considering what your gifts are, try not to think of them in terms of specific roles or job titles but as a unique skill set that can be applied in multiple ways. There may be a particular role you've done for a long time that at some point no longer helps you provide the highest good, but there will be elements of that role that will absolutely help you deliver more value and reap more rewards in the future.

FOUR WAYS TO UNCOVER YOUR GIFTS

If you're ready to start sharing your gifts with the world, making a difference, and enjoying more rewards, it's time to figure out exactly what your gifts are. This is a crucial step to being able to sell without being sales-y, because when you know what your blessing is and you value it, it removes a huge mental stumbling block that most people have about selling—a fear that you're trying to pull one over on the person you're selling to. Remember, selling isn't about being pushy; it's simply about offering your service to help someone you know you can help. And if you aren't clear on your gifts and the value you provide, you'll doubt your ability to help, which will make your offer feel *off*—both to you and the person you're making it to. So let's get you crystal clear on the difference you're here to make and the gifts you bring to the table. To determine what your blessing is, you just have to know how to look for it.

Number 1: Look to Your Life Story

You may think that to do what you want to do, you have to acquire something—a degree, a certain amount of money, or more hours spent honing your craft—but you already have everything you need. You don't need so many letters after your name that they start to wrap around to the back of your business card! You simply have to look back at your life to find the clues that point to what you're here to do.

Before you can move forward toward what you want—that *more* that you can feel you're meant for—it's crucial to take a look back at where you've been. Why? Because you were put on this earth for a reason: a mission that is perfectly designed for you. And everything you've experienced in your life, positive and negative, has taught you what you need to know and has equipped you with the necessary skills for you to complete this mission.

> *Whatever you've lived through, good or bad,*
> *has been the perfect training camp for*
> *where you want to go.*

You've already done the heavy lifting—now it's time to acknowledge just how qualified you already are by looking back and seeing what training camps you've been in.

There is one tricky part to this endeavor. You've got to resist the temptation to look at your life story and feel like a victim. Your challenges make you who you are, and who you are is precisely who you need to be to fulfill your mission. If you feel sorry for yourself about any parts of your story, you won't be able to see the gifts that were wrapped up in whatever you experienced.

For example, during my then-husband Michael's medical residency, we moved every two years. Just as I got settled in a town, found meaningful work, and started building up a network of friends and colleagues, we'd move. One of our moves was to Mexico, where he attended medical school. It was challenging for me because I didn't speak Spanish. I could have had myself a massive pity party. Instead, I used the opportunity to learn Spanish, and also enrolled myself in an international MBA program that was offered in English. Through that program I met some great executives at Hewlett-Packard de Mexico whom I began helping with their online and offline sales presentations—all things that are part of the work my multimillion-dollar international company offers today.

One of my clients and a member of my Sales, Authenticity & Success Business Academy for mission-driven entrepreneurs is Dr. Venus Opal Reese. She is the perfect example of how your life story contributes to the creation and strengthening of your gifts, no matter how traumatic your path may have been.

When she was 16, Venus's mother threw her out of the house. Suddenly homeless, Venus survived by living on the streets of Baltimore amid drugs, pimps, and violence too graphic to share here. One day, Venus sat on the corner she now called home and simply prayed, "God, please help me." The next day, she returned to school. The kids either ran from her ("My odor preceded me," she recalls) or teased her. But her math teacher helped her get cleaned up and gave her a warm meal. This first act of kindness led to a long-term support system that helped Venus find her footing again, and find it she did. Fourteen years later she graduated from Stanford University with two master's degrees and a Ph.D.

Armed with her degrees, Dr. Venus found a job teaching at a university. When her tenure review came up, it was approved, but other members of the faculty voted against her. She says that moment was like being 16 all over again—she felt like she'd been kicked out of the house. And Dr. Venus realized that, despite the fact that she was grateful for the job, she no longer wanted to pretend to be someone she wasn't (or, as she so lovingly puts it, "I got committed to never kissing butt again"). She wanted to help others more deeply than she could from a classroom. That's when she launched her consulting practice and discovered my work to help her get out there with her gift in a much bigger way. What started as a side hustle has now grown into a multi-million-dollar business.

Now Dr. Venus is known as The Millionaire Mentor, and she helps top-performing CEOs and market leaders become the highest-paid leader in their field, live a fulfilling life, and leave a legacy that transforms the world. I promise you, if Dr. Venus can view her early history as a source of strength, you can too.

If your mission has felt elusive thus far—or if you are pretty clear what your mission is, but you haven't figured out how to make it real in the world yet—there are huge clues to be found in your life story. Everything counts. Every setback and triumph taught you exactly what you need in order to make the difference that you were put on this earth to make. By looking back at exactly what type of training camp you have been in, you will see the details of your mission come out of hiding and arrange themselves into a road map.

Exercise: Uncover the Gifts Hidden in Your Story

Get out your notebook and draw a line down the center of the page so that you have two columns, or refer to this exercise in the guide available at www.MeantForMoreGuide.com, and write out the following:

1. In the left-hand column, write down every major (or even not-so-major) challenge that you've lived through—moving a lot as a kid, a health scare, losing weight, bouncing back after a breakup, improving your self-confidence . . . anything you can think of that might fit the bill, jot it down. Also capture your achievements (such as writing a book, revitalizing your health, parenting a child through a particular challenge), as well as all the jobs you've had during your career.

2. In the right-hand column, write down the skills, traits, or talents that you developed as a result of each challenge.

3. Now pretend that you were seeing all this information about a person you had never met before. What conclusions would you draw about this person's aptitudes and capabilities? Write down as many as you can think of—don't hold yourself back. If you notice yourself getting shy here, remind yourself to pretend that you're talking about someone else; it will help you own all the gifts that you've accrued over the years, whether they were factory installed or the result of hard-won experience.

Number 2: Where Do You Meddle?

Another way to tease out your unique blessing is by giving some thought to the situations where you can't help but get involved—in other words, where you meddle.

My client Karen Quinn is a great example of someone whose million-dollar value stems from something she can't *not* do. Karen owns a business that helps kids ace standardized state tests. She started it when her then-four-year-old son scored in the 37th percentile on a state test and his preschool teachers told Karen that she should start looking for special education programs for him to attend. Luckily, Karen's mom was a child education psychologist and she coached Karen on how to work with her son. Those strategies worked—Kevin's next score on a state test was in the 97th percentile. Fast forward eighteen years, and he graduated from NYU.

Driven to share what she learned with other moms, Karen started testingmom.com. It is now a multimillion-dollar business: for about the same cost as one tutoring session, moms can get a yearlong membership to help their kids prepare for these state tests (which most school administrators will tell you your child can't study for). When Karen was recently at my house for a one-on-one business coaching session, we spent two days together doing some pretty intensive work. After one of our breaks, I came back to find her on the computer in the kitchen with my ten-year-old daughter, showing her how to master some of the tougher test questions for an upcoming state test. She "couldn't not" help her. Karen uses her blessing to help thousands of people. She makes a difference every day and she gets paid well to do it.

Exercise: Determine What You "Can't Not" Do

In your notebook or on the worksheet available at www.MeantForMoreGuide.com, ask yourself the following questions:

- What do people come to me for when they need help?

- What do people ask to "pick my brain" about?

- What's hard for others but comes easily to me?

- What is it that I can't *not* do?

- Where do I meddle?

- What frustrates me or drives me crazy when I see it because I know it can be so much better, easier, more efficient, et cetera?

- What do I notice everywhere I go? (For example, every day I see instances in which businesses leave thousands of dollars on the table by not making their offers truly irresistible. A gifted editor might see ways she could tighten the narrative of everything she reads, or a productivity expert might spot all the ways her friends could get more done.)

Whatever your answers are, they'll reveal the areas in which your greatest gifts lie. You get clues every day about what your million-dollar value is—don't dismiss them!

Number 3: Look to People You've Helped

This is more of an externally focused method of identifying your gifts, because it requires you to think about how you have helped other people, rather than looking at your own life or within your own mind. It's a great way to hold a mirror up to your gifts so you can see them objectively. It also helps you articulate them so you can tell others the unique value you have to offer in a clear and compelling way. This empowers you to share your gifts without hesitation—you won't have to get hung up on what to say when you get inspired to offer your help.

Refer back to the "Calculate Your Ripple" exercise in Chapter 3 where you thought of a specific person you've helped—someone who took your advice, ran with it, and had a smashing success as a result, whether they paid you for your time or not. (This person could be you.) Read over the benefits they experienced. And this time, think about how they would describe the following, in their own words:

- What they were struggling with before you helped them
- What they achieved with your assistance

You can do this either by asking them directly or by remembering what they've reported back to you.

For example, if you have a knack for decorating and you helped your friend Martha rearrange her living room, think about how she described what she wanted to do. If she said, "My living room is such a mess I don't even want to go in there," write that down. If she said, "You helped me transform my messy living room into a calm oasis," write that down. Think of everything you can remember her saying about her situation and about the process of working with you, taking care to use the words *she actually used.* Not only will it give you clues about what your particular talents are, this exercise will also provide you with the words you can use to tell people about what you do (this is usually one of the biggest challenges for folks looking to turn their "thing" into an actual product or service).

Number 4: Get Out There and Speak

The final way to reveal your million-dollar value is go out and share from the heart, and then let your audience guide you. You don't need to lead a formal talk—you could authentically share over dinner with your girlfriends or while chatting with your tablemate at a networking breakfast. You can lead from any position in a room—whether that's standing at a podium or sitting in the audience.

Whatever position you're in, there is nothing like being face-to-face with those who need your help to see when their eyes light up. Just as the ocean washes a lumpy, bumpy rock onto the sand and eventually hones it into a smooth, shiny, beautiful stone, the feedback of the people you think you can help can inch you toward where you need to be.

If you're new to public speaking or intimidated by this option in any way, I know how tempting it is to think you need to have all your ducks in a row before you even consider speaking, sharing, presenting—a logo, a website, a business card. Yet you don't have to have everything all figured out in order to start speaking and helping people. When I first started speaking about how to boost sales by making your offer, I had a newborn and a three-year-old and an AOL e-mail address. I wasn't set up to take credit cards. I hadn't even thought of the term "irresistible offer." It didn't matter. I got out there with as much as I was clear on in the moment, and the feedback I got from people gradually nudged me to where I am today.

There are many networking groups that give you a chance to stand up and talk for 30 seconds and tell people what you do. Or now we have the miracle of Facebook or Instagram live, which, with the push of a button, let you talk to and interact with a group of your friends about your passions. Once you start talking to people, you'll see what they respond to the most and what questions they have; this information is priceless, as it helps you see where you can do the most good.

We've developed an entire curriculum to support people who want to use speaking to help more people and make great money doing it. It's called the Speak-to-Sell Formula. It's a system that helps to clarify your irresistible offer and then build a content-rich talk that leads to it. Using speaking to lead to your irresistible offer is a game changer for most start-ups because it allows the presenter to make their offer to more than one person at a time. This is one of the fastest ways to gain confidence and make money while getting out there with your work in its early stages.

Exercise: How to Get Started Speaking

I've included the "108 Places to Speak and Get Clients Guide" in the guide available at www.MeantForMoreGuide.com along with all the worksheets that accompany this book.

Take 10 minutes to access this guide now and pick 10 places where you believe your ideal clientele is already gathering. You may be surprised at how much opportunity already awaits you and feel inspired to book a Speak-to-Sell Signature Talk that helps you develop your irresistible offer. This was the main tool I used to step into my own version of "more" so that I could help clients around the world with my gifts and talents while providing a fabulous lifestyle for my family.

GETTING ON YOUR DIME

I call the process of finding your "thing" and claiming your million-dollar value "getting on your dime." Why? Because a dime is pretty small. It can be hard to find amid a sea of change. And even when you do find it, it can be a challenge to stand on such a small spot. The good news about getting on your dime is that it's like learning how to ride a bike—though it can take a while to nail the balance, once you do, you never forget how to do it. Even if you shift a little to the right or the left, which is natural as you keep learning and growing, once you've learned how to find and stay in your sweet spot, your dime, you'll be able to adjust to any changing conditions that come your way.

Getting on your dime is a process of getting a fuzzy vision of what your "thing" might be and then moving closer and closer to it over time. It's a lifelong journey. Few people are standing right on their dime. Even with the thousands of people I've been able to help, and the millions of dollars I've been able to generate, I'm not totally on my dime. Part of my aim in writing this book is to move closer to it—to stretch myself in ways I haven't before to reach even more people than I've been able to up until this point. And while I have a pretty good idea of what I'm hoping this book will make possible both for you and for me, I also know that you can't always see what your dime is until you start moving toward it—that's when a clearer picture comes into view. The closer you move toward your dime, the more opportunity comes your way. People are more easily able to identify that you're just the help they need, and the heavens part for all the opportunities and abundance that you were put here to receive.

Some of you reading this book have only the faintest glimmer of what your gifts and your million-dollar value are, and some of you have already done a good amount of work at figuring it out and putting it into practice. Either way, you're never totally done with getting on your dime. It's simply not a one-and-done thing. Something will happen and you'll get a bigger vision for yourself; you'll uplevel in some way and then boom, you're back to striving toward your dime.

Think about Oprah—for the many years when her talk show was the most watched daytime show and her book club could launch a writer's career, she was totally on her dime. And then something shifted, and she must have seen a larger purpose for what she could accomplish, causing her to move on to the next phase of running the Oprah Winfrey Network (OWN).

In my case, when I first started my own business, I was thrilled that I could make a six-figure income by teaching entrepreneurs to make irresistible offers. Then the more I worked with people one-on-one and spoke to small audiences and then larger groups, I received the gift of getting feedback about what people really wanted from me. And I found that it went deeper than simply making irresistible offers—people were seeking a way to sell without being sales-y. They wanted to help more people while also being their authentic selves. They needed ways to help people say yes to themselves without feeling like they were being pushy. And I realized that I had a lot of ways to help them do that. The more I wrote those ways down and found out how to communicate them, the more people came to me wanting more. And this is what will happen to you when you start moving toward your dime.

WHERE TO GO FROM HERE

If you are unclear on or uncertain about your blessings, your dime, or the unique transformation you provide, you can do one of two things. First, you can decide to stay confused. Sometimes this is where people need to be. It is simply part of the journey to be unclear at times, a state of mind that varies in length for different people. If that's where you believe you are, honor that.

Your other choice is to admit that you have been confused long enough. You're tired of waiting for your a-ha moment and you're willing to pick a horse and ride it—to get out there with a murky vision of what you're made for, like I did, and start moving forward. It may feel like it's a risky move to get going without a clear plan of exactly what you're going to do first, second, third, fourth, and so on, but I can promise you one thing: When you get into action, the universe will step in and course-correct you as you go. Think of a car with power steering that is parked with the ignition off. If you try to turn the wheels of that parked car right or left, nothing happens. The moment you turn on the ignition and the car starts moving—even if it's very slowly—the power steering kicks in and you can steer with one finger (practically). Just like that car, the surest way for you to stay unclear and stuck is to stand still.

If having an automatic guidance system kick in and help steer you toward your dime sounds pretty darn good right about now, use one of the four ways I shared earlier to discover your gifts. Whichever one you choose, picking one and doing the exercise will get you into motion. We all have to start somewhere. And really, all it takes is that first step to start crystallizing what you have to offer and drawing in the people who can benefit the most from your blessing. Don't leave your people waiting! They need you.

And if you're feeling like you need something more concrete, I've got you covered: In the next chapter, you'll learn how to articulate those gifts clearly, which then draws the people you were meant to help to you.

CHAPTER 5

ASSUME THE THRONE

By now I hope that you have some glimpses, if not an outright vision, of what your unique gifts are. The next step is to articulate them so that the next time someone asks you, "What do you do?" you've got an answer that communicates your million-dollar value.

Telling others about your gifts may feel a little funny at first, as so many of us were never taught to even think of ourselves as special, much less talk about ourselves that way. It's ultimately an empowering act to be able to succinctly communicate what your gifts are. Because as important as it is to be clear on what you have to offer the world, if you don't own those gifts—by telling other people about them and using them in a visible way, in a process I call "assuming the throne"—they will stay hidden and you will not make the difference in the world that you were put here to make.

> *If you don't know how to communicate the transformation you can provide to others, your value will remain a secret.*

This isn't about ego. It's about shining your light, sharing your talents, and claiming your space—and doing it from a place of generosity, compassion, and courage.

STOP WAITING TO BE DISCOVERED

I know what you might be thinking. *If my gifts are so great, shouldn't they be obvious to other people? Do I really have to tell people about them? I thought you said I wouldn't have to be pushy or sales-y!*

Well, if you're not willing to tell people about what you do and how you shine, you're waiting for other people to figure it out. And the longer you wait, the more your talents will stay hidden and the more people won't get the help that you are perfectly designed to deliver.

Waiting to be discovered is such a common trap. We've all heard the stories of the model or actress who was approached by an agent while riding the subway or buying groceries and then went on to mega fame and fortune. Do you know why we all know those stories? Because they're so rare! Meaning, they are so unlikely that when they do happen, we remember them and talk about them for years and years. If you are waiting for someone to send you an e-mail or call you on the phone to say, "You're so amazing, we want to feature you in your own TV show for big bucks!" you will be waiting a long time—possibly for the rest of your life.

Listen, I get it. When I was in my 20s and 30s, working for other people, I knew I had an awesome gift—just as you do. When I was working for Pfizer as a brand-new pharmaceutical rep, I won all the top sales awards, even though many employees had been there years longer than I had. I knew there was something special about the way I helped people and businesses recognize and say yes to opportunities. I figured if I just stayed out there doing my thing long enough, someone would discover me.

When I got to my 40s and no one had knocked on my door saying, "Hey, we heard you're really great at selling and inspiring people, would you like your own TV show? Or to be our keynote speaker?" I realized that I was just going to have to assume the throne.

So I looked at all the various places where I excelled—inspiring people to say yes; crafting and delivering irresistible offers on stages, via teleseminars, and one-on-one; and making people feel seen and heard. I realized that all these different areas that looked so unrelated actually fell under one particular type of transformation—converting prospects into clients.

That's when I dubbed myself the Queen of Sales Conversion. And the funny thing was that no one questioned it. No one said, "Can I see your statistics?" I assumed that throne, put the crown on my own head (and the title on a business card), and no one blinked an eye. Giving myself this expert title was simply a shift in mind-set and in my presentation. When you make this same shift, you'll feel at ease and confident about claiming your own gifts and assuming your throne.

If you want that story of being an average person who made a big splash in the world by using their God-given talents or hard-earned expertise, give it to yourself. Instead of hoping that someone will knock on your door and proclaim you the next big thing, crown yourself with a title that describes what you're best at and shows the world how you are already successful at doing what you do.

GIVE YOURSELF AN EXPERT TITLE

The way you climb up on your throne is to give yourself a title that's accurate and bold. Think of my title: the Queen of Sales Conversion. If it weren't 100 percent true, I'd feel a little funny calling myself the "queen." Since it's an accurate reflection of my natural talents and what I help people do, I wear that moniker with pride. It gives me confidence *and* it helps draw to me the exact people whom I can help the most. It also serves as a North Star to continue to hone my craft.

People are going to be sizing you up and putting you in a category whenever they meet you anyway—it's human nature. By giving yourself a title, you take control of your own messaging. And it's actually a service to other people—because they want to know how to think of you. Giving yourself an expert title answers a lot of questions in other people's minds about who you are and what you have to offer.

Assuming the throne also benefits you in big ways. When you start calling yourself by an expert title, you become that person even more. Some of this is practical: when people know what your expertise is, you will get more problems to solve in that area, which will only boost your skills. And some of it is internal—you will also have higher standards for yourself and you will make an extra effort to keep learning and growing in the role you've claimed for yourself. I'm more interested in and obligated to keep current in sales conversion techniques because of my designation. Giving yourself an expert title creates a self-fulfilling prophecy.

It also helps a person identify himself or herself as someone who needs your help—meaning it lends you what I call "invisible influence." It's a way to sell without being sales-y, because when you do it right, your title will naturally inspire people to say, "Oh, that's what I need!" And if they don't need what you offer in that moment, your title will help them remember what you do, so that when they or someone they know needs what you offer in the future, you'll come to mind. If I know you are the Stress-Free Copywriter, for example, I'll definitely think of you the next time I need help writing something, especially if the thought of doing it myself stresses me out. Or when I talk to someone else who needs writing help, I'll refer them to you.

REPLACE ANY NEGATIVE NOTIONS

It may feel foreign to start calling yourself by a moniker, but you are probably already doing it on some level—and maybe not in the most empowering way. We all have ways we think of ourselves in our heads, whether we actually say them out loud or not. Make sure you actually like the identity you've created for yourself, because as humans, we fight hard to live up to the idea we have of ourselves.

When I was in my 20s and 30s, I called myself the Build-a-Man Workshop. I started dating men when they were just getting started on a career path and supported them through their transformation, and then we would split up just as they became successful. In part, it was a truthful title in that it reflected my past and current relationships at that time; it also impacted my future because those were the types of relationship circumstances I kept creating. Once I was married, I became Mrs. Better Way—and you know by now how well *that* worked out! When I renamed myself the Queen of Sales Conversion, not only did I create a seven-figure business, I upgraded my relationships too.

Giving yourself a new title works in all parts of your life—not just in the areas of your gifts and talents. A few years ago, when I realized this truth, I let go of saying, "I'm an obese person with a ton of discipline," which I used to think was funny, to "I'm petite," which is actually more true and has become truer the longer I've said it!

Isn't it time to let go of the titles that no longer serve you and create some new ones that do? Where might you be able to do that? Can you think of an unofficial title you've crowned yourself with, like my Ms. Better Way or Build-a-Man Workshop? Maybe it's time for an upgrade!

COMING UP WITH YOUR NEW TITLE

So, if you could crown yourself king or queen of some new land, what would it be? What have you been doing for the past 5 years, 10 years, 20 years, or pretty much your entire life (whether you've been paid for it or not)?

You may have a lot of things you're good at, and that's totally okay. The point of this book is to help you hone and name what's calling to you the most right now. By going through the process of distilling your gifts and offering them up for use, you will uncover the one "meant for more" that makes sense of why you're good at all the different things you're good at. See if you can discern the umbrella that encompasses all the gifts you started to unwrap in the last chapter, and brainstorm a title that describes that. If you realize that you didn't quite hit the mark after you've lived with it for a while, you can refine it later.

It helps to focus on what transformation you are ultimately creating for people. It's also useful to identify the audience you serve. Ideally, you want your title to speak both the *what* you offer as well as the *who(m)* you offer it to.

It's important that your title use very simple language—words that the people who need your gifts would actually say. A way to tease out these words is to think about what people say about you. Do they tell you you're so Zen because you help them calm down when they're upset about something? Or do they say, "It's like you're my therapist?" Do your friends compliment you on your delicious, healthy meals? Really think about the words people are already using to describe you and the outcomes you create in the world.

One of my clients who is also my stylist calls herself an "image therapist" because she helps people feel better about the way they look and how they think about and present themselves. Dr. Venus Opal Reese, whose story I shared in Chapter 4, gave herself the title The Millionaire Mentor, which immediately lets you know who her clientele is and what it is she does. Another client, a former ER doctor, gave himself the title of End of Life Empowerment Specialist, so people who are feeling like they are at the mercy of the system as they near the end of their lives—or their loved one's life—can immediately identify themselves as a person who needs his help. The more your words that reflect the reality of the people you're meant to help, the better.

If you're working for another company, you can still choose your own title. You could start referring to yourself as a "client happiness specialist" even though it may still say that your title is Head of Returns on the org chart and your business card. If your title is Account Manager, you could call yourself a "partner concierge"—it will change the way you show up and are seen at work, I promise you.

As you think about your new title, here are some guidelines to keep in mind.

- **Don't sacrifice effective for cutesy.** Maybe your mom used to call you an adorable pet name, or you got a nickname in high school that stuck, or you started blogging 10 years ago with a funny title—those are not going to help you assume the throne. Remember, your focus is on your expertise and the transformation you offer. While you do want it to be memorable, you want it to stick in people's minds because it tells them how you can help them, not because it's cute or silly.

- **Be as clear as possible.** If you have to do a lot of explaining after you say your title—your moniker is three words but you have to say three paragraphs after it to really say what it means—you probably need an upgrade. Pay close attention to the words you say to describe what you do *after* you say your expert title. In almost every case the better title is hiding in plain sight in those three paragraphs that really describe what you do.

- **Embrace your expertise.** Make sure your new title lets the world know that you are good at what you do. Words people often use are *expert, guru, mentor,* and *specialist.*

- **Don't let self-judgment keep you from going for it.** Remember that it's okay to choose an area of expertise that you're still developing. Although my title was 100 percent accurate when I initially chose it, I'm much more the queen of sales conversion now than I was 10 years ago.

GETTING COMFORTABLE WITH YOUR NEW TITLE

As long as you come up with a name that inspires you, you can't mess this up. Just pick a horse and ride it. You may not choose a title that completely sums you up forevermore, but it will get you moving and showing up in the world in a different way. And that's when more insight and information about your gifts and what's possible for you will be revealed.

If you start to doubt yourself, refer back to the costs of people *not* accepting your offer (from the Calculate Your Ripple exercise on page 37). Remember, it's your land—you created it—and it's your opportunity to step up and claim your throne. You wouldn't have crowned yourself if you didn't have sufficient powers in that area.

> *The point of assuming the throne is that you stop waiting for someone else to discover you. Go ahead and take your seat at the head of table.*

There's another aspect of giving yourself an expert title that is incredibly beneficial—accountability to yourself. A few years ago, I had two students in the online version of my Speak-to-Sell Bootcamp who were writing a book together called *No One's the Bitch*. One of the women is the current wife of the other's ex-husband, and together they co-parent two children. It's a scenario that's often filled with name-calling and casting blame. Yet because these two women are teaching these courses and writing that book, they have to keep working on their relationship and keep it positive for themselves, the kids, and all the women they serve. Being willing to be a spokesperson and role model of something you care about requires you to stay aligned with what you teach.

Whatever you choose, and however you choose to share it, approach it as if you're trying on a new coat. Wear it for a while and see how it feels. Does it empower you, excite you, lift you up, or make you blush a bit? You should feel a little rush of energy; that zing tells you you're on to something that's true and stretching yourself to grow in a positive way.

How your title should *not* make you feel is yucky in any way. Although it may feel a little uncomfortable or unfamiliar at first, it should not make you feel bad about yourself. Make sure your expert title authentically represents who you are because then you won't feel like you're bragging or being untruthful. In fact, people will be happy and relieved for you that you're finally owning it. You'll know you're on to something when people are excited for you, as it's often easier for other people to recognize your gifts than it is for you to see them yourself. And it's such a relief for everyone when you have the moment of enlightenment that inspires you to claim your expertise!

Exercise: Craft Your Expert Title

- Name the outcome, benefit, or transformation that you provide. If you help people market themselves on social media in a way that's painless and powerful, the outcome is "powerful but painless social media." If you are a professional organizer, the benefit you provide is "spaces that support you instead of stress you out." Write down a few different versions of your benefits and transformation, and if you get stuck, just keep it simple. You could also just write down "social media" or "home organization"—sometimes simplest is best.

- Then choose an expert title that speaks to you and that describes what you do. Possibilities include: specialist, expert, queen, king, leader, leading authority, America's #1, wizard, whiz, genius, strategist, guide, authority, maven, mentor, coach, and pro.

- Now put the two together: The Powerful and Painless Social Media Maven. The Queen of Organized Spaces.

- Voilà! Take the version you like the most and try it on for size. Add it to your e-mail signature, put it on a set of free business cards, use it in your introduction at the next networking meeting you attend. Check to make sure that you feel connected to it before committing.

You'll find this exercise outlined in the worksheets available at www.MeantForMoreGuide.com. There you'll also find a list of others' expert titles for inspiration and a longer list of possible descriptors.

STEP THREE

GET INTO ACTION

Before we move into this next section, I just want to take a moment to remind you that the Meant for More Formula is a *system*. I've spent years paying attention to the steps one has to take to have a bigger impact and the best order in which to accomplish those steps.

By now your million-dollar value should be starting to reveal itself. If you're not yet 100 percent certain about it, that's OK. This next step of the formula will help you take your new insights—even if they're still forming—and put them into action. And action is what will help you get on your dime.

In the last chapter, we covered how to assume the throne by giving yourself an expert title, which is a key part of being able to get what you're worth—after all, if you're not willing to tell people the transformation you deliver, how can you expect them to value what you offer? That step came before this one because I wanted you to start stepping into your own expertise before you start taking action. Because when you have clarity about the value you bring to the table, you're more likely to take steps that will actually move you forward and call you to live into your highest vision of yourself.

There are three different types of action you'll embrace in this section: inspired action, decisive action, and imperfect action.

While they are all slightly different from one another, they all lead to what I call "forward momentum." I'm sure you know someone who stays busy all day long yet never really seems to move any closer to their goals—or perhaps you've had that experience. There's lots of movement, but you're not getting anywhere . . . kind of like jumping up and down. The types of action you will discover in the upcoming chapters help propel you forward and take new ground. In addition to helping you get on your dime, I think you'll quickly see that it's a very invigorating way to live!

CHAPTER 6

TAKE INSPIRED ACTION

As someone who has had the privilege to coach and mentor thousands of people, a common complaint that I hear from folks—sometimes in reference to their business growth, sometimes in terms of their own personal development—is that they are frustrated with how long it has been taking them to make the changes they are longing to make.

The way out of impatience is to take action. Because action creates results. That's why this and the next two chapters focus on different kinds of action you can take.

You can't just think your way into growing and transforming and having a different reality. If you've been futzing with your resume and commiserating with your coworkers but haven't actually gone on any interviews, it's no surprise that you aren't in a job you like yet.

Sure, mind-set plays a huge role in success, but ultimately, if you never take tangible steps, things won't change.

> *The best way to accelerate your growth*
> *is to start taking inspired action.*

When I say inspired action, I'm talking about the moves you make as a result of trusting those insights and impulses that come from a higher place. The quicker you start moving on your inspirations, the quicker you'll get results that delight you.

I know you get inspired ideas every day. The question is, when you have the thought, do you do the action? When you get the e-mail from a friend telling you why she's participating in a walkathon and her story touches your heart, do you actually click the "donate now" button? Or do you put it off?

I know that we've all been taught that it's important to weigh decisions carefully, but analyzing and measuring every move doesn't always serve us. Why? Because the door of possibility that you sense when that inspiration comes along only stays open for a very brief time. One minute the possibility feels so real; the next it has vanished. That's how quickly opportunity can, and usually does, disappear . . . *if* there's not a structure and action in place to keep it alive.

The more distance you get from an inspired idea, the more likely it is that all the excuses will start coming in, including thoughts like, *I should really talk to my husband first* or *I'm not sure if this is the right next step.* If you wait to donate until after the kids go to bed, your inner voice will have a chance to chime in and tell you that the $100 should probably go toward your credit card, and what difference will just $100 make anyway . . . and are they really doing good things with the money? It goes on and on.

The dialogue inside your head that tries to talk you out of your inspired ideas is something I call resistance. Although people often take resistance as a sign that they shouldn't do what they've gotten the call to do, the thoughts that come from resistance aren't necessarily the truth. They're an equal and opposite reaction to the inspired thinking that triggered them.

To deal with resistance more skillfully, you've got to thank that naysaying voice for sharing, and then get back to the inspired thought. (I talk more about resistance in Chapter 12, so if that feels hard to do, don't panic! You'll get more support on dealing with doubts soon.)

I believe inspiration comes straight from God, the universe, the divine, your trusted source—whatever you want to call the higher intelligence that infuses everything. It's your Great Me talking, which, remember, is another way of referring to your heart. Resistance, on the other hand, comes from the Little Me, otherwise known as your head. Which one do you want to honor? And which one do you think is going to produce better results?

Acting on your inspirations is a tangible way to put your heart in the driver's seat. Making pros and cons lists, polling your friends, and sleeping on decisions are often not of service, because they create just enough time for the door of possibility to close.

On the other hand, when you act on your inspiration, miracles happen. Here's just one little example. While I was in the middle of writing this book, I led a three-day event. When I got home, I was wiped out. I was lying in bed having a tough time starting my day when I noticed myself thinking about a friend and colleague named Mary Morrissey. I knew I was going to see her at another event later in the week, so I decided to trust that I was thinking about her for a reason and texted her to see if we could get together for dinner at that event. She responded right away (and Mary has a thriving business with plenty of things vying for her attention). She said, "I woke up thinking of you too. Do you have time to talk right now for a few minutes?" I did, and on that phone call, she gave me some advice that spoke straight to my heart, addressed a few things that were weighing heavy on me, and got me feeling ready to get up and get back to making the difference I was put here to make.

The kicker is we could have tried for six months to find a time to talk and not found one. Or if we had found a time, by the time that meeting came around, I wouldn't have needed to hear those exact words she gifted me with that morning. Because I followed my inspiration and we ended up getting on the phone so quickly, I didn't have time to get in my head and prepare for the call. In fact, I was still in bed when we spoke! I was able to be vulnerable. And as a result, she poured into me the most perfect, loving advice that I needed at just that moment. And that is the magic of inspired action.

This magic works both ways, though, and that's why you definitely want to catch it on the upswing! Because if you keep getting an inspiration—that you want to share your expertise, maybe start a business and do work you're passionate about, or you feel called to improve your relationship—and you keep shoving it down, you're going to get called into action in a much more shocking way. Again, if you don't take the tap, you're going to get the 2 x 4. All those little bubblings-up of inspiration are the taps. If you keep ignoring them, they're going to stop being so gentle. You're much more likely to get a 2 x 4—the car accident, the firing, or the divorce that stops you in your tracks and forces you to switch gears. Although I believe that everything that happens in our life ultimately serves us, I'd still rather take the taps than the smacks upside the head, wouldn't you?

Here's an example of how honoring the tap can create magic in your life and help you avoid the 2 x 4—for you and your family. My daughter Sierra had been a competitive gymnast for five years. At 10 years old, she was ready to move up a level in the competitions and start doing some of the trickier moves.

One day, seemingly out of the blue, Sierra looked in my eyes and told me that she wanted to stop doing gymnastics and switch over to dance. At first I was confused—had something happened that had discouraged her? Was this a moment where I should teach her a lesson in perseverance?

As soon as Sierra explained why she wanted to switch, I understood. She had gotten an inspiration that she could take the skills she'd built as a gymnast and transition into dance. She felt that now was the time to make the switch, because if she waited another year, it would be that much harder to catch up to the kids who had been dancing since they were five.

I started investigating, and we discovered that every girl in her gymnastics troupe who was a level above her had broken at least two major bones (because they had started incorporating back flips and tricky jumps into their routines). Every single one. Sierra was moved to make the switch from inspiration. Looking at it more closely, we could see that there was a very good chance that if we ignored that tap—if I had tried to have a "don't quit" parenting moment—the 2 x 4 was very likely to involve bodily harm. Now, I'm happy to report, she's on two dance teams, and the owner of the dance studio can't believe she's never danced before. Plus, the six-hour-a-week dance schedule is much more manageable than the 30-hour-a-week gymnastics schedule—which proved to be a total blessing as she started her first year of middle school just a few months after making the switch. This is the kind of good outcome that's available to you when you listen to the taps and then take inspired action!

I know that acting on your inspirations can trigger that voice inside your head that always wants to keep you safe. I've got a formula to help you get around it.

LISTEN, ACT, TRUST

Even though the Meant for More Formula is a system in itself, it has minisystems built into it. There's even a formula for acting on inspiration! I call it Listen, Act, Trust, and it works like this:

- **Listen:** The first step in the formula isn't so much of a step as it is a softening. You've got to be receptive to hearing and acknowledging those thoughts that come from a higher place. It's also about what you *don't* want to do, which is dismiss those ideas that come to you in your quiet moments.

  The only thing to keep in mind here is that you want to listen to the ideas that lift you up and create good for everyone—including you. So I'm not advocating that you listen to every impulse, like keying someone's car or flying into a road rage when someone cuts you off. Those impulses are more in the category of reaction than of inspiration. I have a sign on my desk from an improv class that says, "Always add." The inspirations worth listening to and acting on add to the world, not detract from it.

81

- **Act:** Take some action on the inspiration as quickly as you can. The bigger the gap between getting the idea and acting on the idea, the lower the likelihood that you will do it, because, remember, the door of possibility closes pretty quickly. Taking some action props that door open for a longer time. Commit to an action that gets you enrolled in some kind of structure—whether that's finding a coaching mastermind, a book club, or a nanny you can book for every other Saturday night. The structure holds open the possibility and helps you create more freedom in your life, because you won't constantly have to decide what you're going to do—you simply follow the structure you put in place. And that saves tons of mental energy and time!

- **Trust:** This can be the hardest part for a lot of people—I promise, it will get easier the more you do it. Here I'm talking about trusting that your inspiration was actually helpful. It's so common that we listen, we act, and then we start doubting ourselves, getting second opinions, second guessing . . . all of which are killers of the possibility you just created by taking that inspired action! You've got to trust that if you were inspired, your heart is leading you someplace good, and it's usually something you just can't see yet from where you stand. In order to access that trust, it helps to think of yourself as committed but not attached—you're committed to taking action, but you're not attached to any specific outcome. In this way, you stay open to the unexpected (perhaps there's an even better outcome than what you can imagine!). You also start to practice a principle that will provide you with a lot of clarity and peace when making your irresistible offer (which we'll cover in Chapter 10).

BUILDING THE CYCLE OF TRUST

The more you start to act on the inner knowing of your heart (instead of the research and rationalizations of your head), the more you will start to trust your inspirations. That trust will make it easier for you to "listen, act, trust" the next time inspiration hits.

I want to be clear: I'm not saying you should never do any research or consult other people who are impacted by your decisions. I'm merely pointing out that you can subconsciously use research and inquiry as a delay tactic, one that can keep you from experiencing incredible growth and rewards. It's human nature to try to put off making decisions; you have to train yourself to break this natural tendency.

When you start to incorporate "listen, act, trust" into your daily life and close the gap between the listen and the act, you'll make better decisions, receive more transformations, and learn to trust your inspirations.

One of my favorite quotes is from Maxwell Maltz, a Columbia University–educated medical doctor who wrote *Psycho-Cybernetics* in 1960—a book designed to help people overcome limiting beliefs that was a forerunner of the self-help movement. He wrote:

> *A step in the wrong direction is better than staying on the spot all our life. Once you're moving forward you can correct your course as you go. Your automatic guidance system cannot guide you when you're standing still.*

To me, this quote is all about using inspired action to deepen your relationship with your inner knowing—or what he calls your automatic guidance system (decades before GPS and Google Maps!)—and moving toward your goals even when you don't feel like you've got the route all mapped out in advance.

At my live training events that I host twice a year, I teach as much as I can fit into those three days, and then I make an irresistible offer to those folks who are loving what they're hearing and wanting more personal attention and accountability to join my yearlong mastermind and mentorship program. If you could stand on the stage with me and see what I can see on people's faces when they're in that gap between having the inspiration to say yes to themselves and cycling through all the reasons why they "shouldn't" join my program, you'd be astonished. Their faces are grayed out, as if they are wearing veils. After they've decided to make the leap, they look brighter, uplifted, and 10 years younger. If you could see how (visibly) indecision affects you, you would run toward whatever action is calling to your heart!

It's common to think that you have to wait for confidence or clarity before you act. The irony is that, confidence and clarity come when you honor your inspiration. If you find yourself thinking, "I'm going to wait until I get clearer," you may never get that certainty because it's the reverse—when you take an action, you get feedback and an opportunity to grow your capabilities, and that builds your confidence and your clarity. The more you get in the habit of acting on your inspirations, the more proof you get that you're on the right path. It's a positive feedback loop that creates a cycle of trust.

Exercise: Write Your Own Headlines

In life and in business, you can help yourself make more decisions from your heart by writing the headlines you want to be written for the story of your life.

Here's an example: When my ex-husband, who is the father of my two kids, and I were in the process of getting divorced, there were many moments when I had to choose a course of action that would likely determine the kind of relationship we would have post-divorce. I have a ton of love and appreciation for the path that my now-ex and I shared, and he and I are committed co-parents and will be for the rest of our lives. Still, I had moments during our divorce when I felt a strong urge to squash him like a bug. I'm sure he had similar moments with me too. That's when I'd think of the headline that I had written in my head about the story I wanted to tell when I looked back on our relationship: "La Jolla Heart Surgeon and *Inc.* 500 CEO Develop Collaborative Divorce Arrangement to Co-Parent Kids to Success." It helped me make choices that got me exactly where I wanted to go: in a collaborative and communicative relationship, making choices that are in the best interests of our children.

There are a couple of key points to keep in mind as you write the headline for the outcome you want. The most important is that you want to be focused on creating a result that delivers the highest good for all concerned . . . including you. It's not about you trying to get one over on someone else or you taking one for the team. You want the end that you're aiming for to be for the highest good for *all.* The headline I wrote about my divorce is a good example of this. It reflects a positive outcome for everyone involved: my ex, our kids, and me. When you envision the end you're aiming for, aim high. While our relationship still has a way to go to live up to that headline, it's a great North Star to help guide my choices and reactions.

If you are making plans to deliver your first talk, for example, write yourself a headline like "Rising Entrepreneur Helps Others Succeed at the Things They Care About Most." Or if you're trying to effect change within your company, try something like "Passionate Intrepreneur Helps Company Grow by Offering Insights and Building Consensus."

Here are the steps I use to write an inspiring headline. (Record your thoughts and answers in your trusty journal or in the worksheet available at www.MeantForMoreGuide.com):

Step 1: Think about how you want this particular story to turn out. Make your desired outcome a win-win for everyone involved—because that will inspire you to make decisions from your heart instead of your head.

Step 2: Now imagine that you've come to the end of this particular circumstance and someone is writing an article about your journey. What would you want the headline to say?

Step 3. Once you write your headline, use it daily as a decision-making filter. If you have a couple of minutes of free time on a Saturday afternoon, think of your headline and ask,

What could I do that would bring me closer to the outcome I want? At every crossroads, ask, *If this is the headline I'm going for, what action serves that outcome best?*

One note of caution about writing your headlines:

In my early years I did a lot of assisting and supporting of leaders with missions I believed in. I was doing it in part because I wanted to be a leader. So I took actions consistent with the headline I didn't even realize I had written but was aiming for nonetheless: "Star Employee Ascends to the Role of CEO." As a result of that headline, I worked hard to impress the leader and tried to be as much like them as I could. Ironically, I always rose just high enough to become the sidekick to the leader. I didn't realize that I had focused on a headline that had me trying to be someone else!

Once I decided that the headline I really wanted was more along the lines of "Mission-Driven Sales Whiz Uses Her Gifts to Make a Difference in the World," I looked up and realized that people were following *me*. My path to become the leader I'd always wanted to be came from focusing my headline on using my gifts and making a difference—not on being a leader.

I learned the hard way that to be a leader, you have to focus on the transformation you want to provide for others.

ANGELS COME IN MANY FORMS

Sometimes your inspirations will come from other people—a conversation with a friend, like the one I had with Mary, or someone you plop down next to at a networking event. It might even be someone who makes you mad or upset, where the interaction teaches you something or shows you a change you need to make that ends up making all the difference for you. I like to think of those people as your angels. They are everywhere if you look—and as you get more comfortable with listening, acting, and trusting you will start to notice them more.

It may not even be a particular person that triggers your inspiration—it could be an event or a challenge. The principle to remember is that angels come in many forms. There are so many opportunities to experience inspiration if you let yourself.

I encountered an angel recently when my team and I decided to submit an application to Ernst & Young to be considered for the Entrepreneur of the Year award in San Diego. Although we had applied once in the past, this year our revenue had grown 35 percent, and we got accepted to the semifinals.

As part of the process, Ernst & Young sends auditors to your office to look at your books. Most of the other 28 companies in the semifinal round were big biotech firms with fancy offices. To audit our books, they had to come to my home office. As if that was intimidating enough, I speak a different language than they do. They're a big corporate consulting firm, and I talk about serving mission-driven entrepreneurs. While I had every confidence in our numbers, I could tell that they were listening for something that I was just not articulating. When they left, I wasn't feeling great about our chances. And when I thought about the next step in the process—12 different interviews with 12 different judges to be held in two weeks—I was nervous.

The next day, I left for vacation with some of my dearest friends, who are also entrepreneurs in the coaching, training, and online marketing space. Being away from home, surrounded by big thinkers, I started to see what I do in a different way. Now, for a year up until this point, I'd been searching for a bigger vision—a way to think about what I do beyond just being an online training company. I was sitting by the pool when it came to me: we are reducing the failure rate of startups by having them be profitable fast, so they can make the difference they started up for. Now, this isn't any different from what we'd been doing all along, it was just a different way of looking at it and talking about it. Getting out of my daily routine helped me see what was already there.

The discomfort of that audit was my angel. It got me to think differently and helped me go in to those interviews and share what we're truly up to. I told them, "I'm helping entrepreneurs get profitable fast, so they can be sitting in this chair; you'll have so many more applicants because of us." I could see by the light in their eyes that they got it. When I was in their offices, I got a selfie with the Entrepreneur of the Year trophy and got it in my cells what it feels like to have that honor. It almost didn't matter that we didn't win; we'd made it farther than we ever had before, and I got an inspiring vision that helps me think bigger about what we do and stay excited about continuing to improve our offerings.

As you start to implement "listen, act, trust," be sure to watch out for your angels! They are everywhere.

Exercise: Commit to a Daily Stretch

I want to give you a framework for making sure that you stay on track with taking inspired action consistently so that you start to experience the momentum it builds right away. And that framework is an exercise I call the Daily Stretch.

Here's how to do it:

Step 1: Every single day, I want you to ask yourself, "What could I do to stretch myself today? What will help me move toward my vision of my Meant for More?"

Even if the vision of what you're moving toward is still forming, go with what you know for now—the truth is, you never stop evolving and you can always inch closer to your dime, so resist the urge to wait until you get it just right! (You'll learn more about how to embrace the freedom of imperfection in Chapter 8.)

Step 2: Trust that whatever answer you hear—even a seemingly random thought—is coming from your inspiration.

Step 3: Do the thing your inspiration is telling you to do.

In many cases the most powerful stretch is to do that one thing that you've been unwilling to do. Perhaps you've been wanting to get healthier and you know that keeping a food journal would help you make better food choices, but you've been waiting until a better time—*that* would be a perfect stretch to undertake that day. It could also be someone to call, an e-mail to respond to, a decision to make, or a difficult conversation that needs to be broached.

Step 4: If nothing comes to mind, ask yourself, "What's something I can do today to be generous? Or compassionate? Or courageous?"

Acting on any of these guiding principles will naturally help you move toward your "more."

CHAPTER 7

CULTIVATE DECISIVENESS

As important as it is for you to follow your heart and act on your inspiration, you also need to cultivate the ability to take action even when inspiration isn't present or obvious to you. Because as powerful as inspiration is, unfortunately, it isn't a constant. There will be times you need to make a choice even when your heart isn't sending a clear message about what you want in that moment.

These types of decisions tend to be more of the everyday variety—what to do with the free hour you have until your next meeting, whether to accept an invitation, or what to say in response to a particular e-mail. Even though they're smaller, these everyday decisions play a big role in creating your energy and momentum.

The decisions you make every day shape the story you will eventually tell about your relationship, your business, your family, and your life. Although it may seem like a little thing, avoiding making even tiny decisions sets the stage for you to feel like you don't have a say in how the story of your life gets written. You basically put yourself in a position of waiting for other people or circumstances to make your decisions for you. Leave too many decisions unmade, and you scatter your energy and invite more indecision into your life. You become reactive instead of being proactive.

Taking decisive action is your way up and out of that place of feeling stuck or frozen. When you cultivate the habit of being decisive—even when you aren't able to tap into inspiration—you'll put yourself on the fast path to extraordinary rewards.

Becoming more decisive helps you create three important benefits for yourself:

- **Gets you into action.** Here's an analogy: If you're a woman at a club and a man asks you to dance and you say yes, then you're dancing. You're in it. Your decision to accept his offer puts you both into action. Although it may seem impolite, saying no is also great—that way the guy can go ask someone else. If you say maybe, or let me think about it, you're both stuck—should he stick around? Leave and come back? It puts everyone in a holding pattern, and not a very enjoyable one at that. The pain of indecision is just as true in all the other parts of your life as it is on the dance floor. When you make a decision, you and the people impacted by your decision become free to move forward. And every action you take gives you feedback that helps you make your next decision. Remember, you can course-correct as you go, but you can't make any progress when you're standing still.

- **Opens the door to transformation.** All transformation is preceded by a decision. You don't just wake up one day as a different person. Anytime you've experienced growth there was something that you made a decision about beforehand—you decided to go to the party the night you met your partner, or you resolved to change careers after you got laid off. And because you have that knowing that you're meant for more, you need to help other people come to a decision too so that they can experience their own transformation. We'll cover exactly how to help others be more decisive in Step Four. For right now, just know that the more decisive you can be, the more transformation you'll be able to create, both for yourself and for others.

- **Creates your karma.** It's a universal truth that what you put out into the world influences what you get back. Have you ever noticed that when you're being generous, you get a lot of generosity coming back? Or when you're being critical of your spouse you get into a lot of fights? For six years, I taught workshops on relationships. So often, a woman would come in to the workshop feeling like she needed to fix her man because he wasn't listening and not putting her first. When she really stopped and took a look at what was happening, she'd see that he was never able to get a word in edgewise. She would realize that she wasn't listening to him, and in many cases, she was putting him last, after the kids and a whole list of other things. When she changed her actions, time and time again she'd see that her Prince Charming was right there, under her nose, and had been there all along. It's essentially the golden rule—treat others as you would like to be treated, and they will treat you better too. Being decisive will help those around you be decisive too; this will come in handy when you start making irresistible offers (which we'll cover in Step Four).

DECISIVE ACTION HELPS YOU BE THE KIND OF PERSON YOU WANT TO ATTRACT

If you're the type who buys an outfit at Nordstrom, uses it for a photo shoot, and then returns it, you can't be surprised if you're experiencing a lot of clients who request a refund. It's true in your personal life too: If you have a pile of forms you need to get back to your kid's school and e-mails from friends asking to get together that you haven't responded to, you can't be surprised when no one RSVPs to your party. Whatever results you are getting that you don't like, take an honest look in the mirror. Where are you guilty as charged? Use your decisions from here on out to be the kind of person you want to attract into your life.

In 2014, we were launching an online product we had launched successfully many times before; but this time around, people weren't buying. We checked our messaging and tested our links, and it wasn't a glitch in the system. I decided to do an automatic writing exercise, as I described in Chapter 2, to ask my Trusted Source, God, what was going on. The answer I got was this: "How can you ask people to respond to you decisively if you have so many open loops?" I looked through my inbox and saw a slew of invitations for speaking events, fundraisers, dinners, and more that I hadn't answered. I had a lot of "let's do lunch" going on in my life—lots of maybes and lots of vagueness. I spent some time over the next few days responding to all those invitations, saying either "No, but thank you so much," or "Great, here are a few dates to choose from." Then we relaunched the same promotion, and you guessed it—we had our usual rate of sign-ups once again.

The simple truth is, if you want better results in your life, you've got to be decisive. And because decisions are so powerful, you can use them to help create the results that you want. If you want people to take you seriously, take yourself seriously. If you want people to invest in you, invest in yourself. If you want to feel appreciated, appreciate others. If you want people to stop responding to your offers with "I'll think about it," start being decisive when you are faced with an offer or invitation.

Decisiveness does take courage, because committing to a course of action means that you are saying no to some of your other options. The Latin root of the word "decide" means to "cut off" or "cut away." And taking options off your plate can feel like a scary thing do. The good news is that you can strengthen your decision-making muscles so that it doesn't feel as scary. I've got an exercise that will help you do just that coming up on page 96.

A member of my mentorship program, Jenean Merkel Perelstein, has a perfect story to demonstrate the power of making decisions—even ones that feel a little reckless at first. For the first few years she was in business as a women's leadership coach, Jenean worked out of her house. While she had a few clients and was helping them achieve impressive results—getting promotions, earning more money—her business was, in her words, "mediocre." She was making $18,000 a year.

Then a friend invited Jenean to share an office space with her. Jenean's rational mind said she wouldn't get a good return on her investment—after all, she had a perfectly serviceable home office. Even though there were piles of laundry in the corner, it had a desk, a computer, and a phone. But Jenean's inner wisdom told her that committing to the expense of rent would force her to take her business more seriously. She knew that if she was truly committed to being in business and being seen as a leader, the decision made a ton of sense. "I knew if I let this decision pass me by and listened to the stories in my head about how I never follow through on things, I was going to keep letting other opportunities go by me too." Thinking of how much she'd regret *not* taking her business seriously outweighed the fear of spending the money on rent.

So she said yes. And almost the minute she signed the lease papers, Jenean's business expanded to fill the space that she provided it. "I started taking myself more seriously, and so did other people," she recalls. Her confidence and her ownership soared. And now, three years later, she reports that she just crossed the six-figure mark only a few months into the year.

Being decisive works in your personal life too. Zarinah El-Amin Naeem, one of our amazing members who leads women on transformative trips abroad, lives in Detroit. When she was traveling to Denver, Zarinah decided to reach out to a Facebook-only friend who lives there to go out for coffee during her visit. Once these two women got together, they hit it off right away. And Zarinah discovered that her new friend is considering a move to Detroit, meaning they'll have many more chances to keep developing their friendship in real life even after the trip is over.

I'm guessing you know just how wonderful and rare it is to make true new friends as an adult—Zarinah herself says it's "amazing to have a new sister in my network, all because I took a chance on a stranger."

Remember, all transformation is preceded by a decision. And whether that transformation is making more money or making a new friend, it's choosing a course of action that makes it possible.

Exercise: Close Your Open Loops

I use this technique in my own life as well as teach it to my clients, and it never fails to get things moving. To do it:

Go through your e-mail, your texts, your stack of mail, and the piles of things in your house that need your attention and make decisions about anything that needs your input.

You don't necessarily have to say yes to everything; responding no is just as powerful.

This isn't about being virtuous; it's about creating clarity and sending that out into the world so that you also invite clarity back into your life. If a friend has sent you a text about getting together and that's something you want to do, you don't just write back, "Sounds great!" You suggest two or three dates that work for you so you can get it on the calendar and close that loop. If you know you don't intend to get together with that person, you reply by thanking them and letting them know that it's just not something you can do right now, and that you'll be back in touch when the timing is better.

Closing open loops is a beautiful gift to you and the receiver. They now know where they stand—they can count you in for their party, or free up their calendar, or take you off their Christmas card list. It's the "maybes" in life that kill possibility and keep everyone stuck. In this way, being decisive is also a compassionate thing to do, because it gets the person who is waiting for your answer out of limbo; and it's generous, because it helps the other person get into action for themselves.

Those open loops may not have someone else associated with them—they might be right in your own house. Every once in a while, I have so many open loops just in my bedroom— unreturned shoes from Zappos, a pile of things to go to the dry cleaner, broken jewelry, kid stuff in the corner, my closet feeling completely unorganized—that I'll sacrifice a couple hours of sleep just to wake up to the feeling of completion. While I am a huge proponent of getting plenty of rest, sometimes I know that I'll get more peace staying up an extra hour or two and closing all those open loops, and will wake up feeling clearer and more energized. That's the beauty of training yourself to make more decisions quicker—it not only propels you forward, it feels great.

WHAT'S KEEPING YOU FROM BEING DECISIVE?

As powerful as cultivating decisiveness is, if it were totally easy, I wouldn't need to dedicate a whole chapter in this book to doing it! It's so common to get stuck in indecision mode. I want to take a moment to address the most common stalling techniques so you can identify where you get hung up. You can use this insight to get out of your own way and clear the path to your "more."

- **Researching ad nauseam.** It's one thing to be an educated consumer. Nobody likes overpaying or spending money on things that don't serve us. But if every possibility you consider dies in the research phase, it's time to start leaning on the Listen, Act, Trust formula you learned in Chapter 6. At some point you have to make your best guess and go with it. Make it your goal to get faster at closing the loop!

- **Polling others.** There's nothing wrong with wanting to talk out an opportunity so that you can verbally process your options. Just remember that, most likely, the person you're going to talk to about it probably wasn't there to hear what the offer or opportunity actually entails. Even if they were, they're not you—they have different gifts, values, goals, and resources. It may be the perfect next step for you to spend a couple thousand dollars for a certification or online training, but they wouldn't pay more than $15 for a book—of course they're going to think you're crazy.

When I turned 40, I invested in a $100,000 year-long entrepreneurial training mentorship, and at the time, my husband and I definitely did *not* have that money under our mattress. Michael was still in his medical residency and our kids were 3 and 1. When I asked my CPA about it, she thought I was crazy. Thank God my husband believed in me and told me to go for it, because that was the catalyst to everything I've done since. In that first year, I went from earning about $100,000 a year coaching clients one-by-one to selling over $2 million of my own training products and services! I knew that if I wanted others to invest in me, I needed to invest in myself, so after I had that conversation with my CPA, I shut down any more conversation about it, trusted my gut, and leapt. (And am I ever glad I did!)

- **Not trusting yourself.** This is what's actually at the heart of all the researching and polling. Usually not trusting yourself comes from a time you let yourself down in the past. If you keep using that mistake as an excuse, you know what your future is going to be—it's going to be more of your past. At some point you've got to forgive yourself. You did the best that you could at that time. You're at a different place now, and it's time to give yourself another chance. Price Pritchett, the author of one of my favorite books, *You²*, writes that it's not about taking a chance; it's about *giving* yourself a chance. I've come to see over and over that you truly are your best investment.

- **Feeling like you need permission.** This is such a common one, you may be falling prey to this stall tactic and not even know it: So many of the women I talk to and work with feel like they need to get permission from someone else—their husband, their accountant, their kids—in order to do what their heart is telling them to do. The truth is, the permission you're looking for needs to come from you.

Tapping into your inner well of courage will get you through all stall tactics. It will also help with one more common reason why people put off making decisions—and that's a fear of not getting things right, otherwise known as perfectionism. Read on to learn about how to embrace the idea of going forward with "good enough."

CHAPTER 8

GET PAST PERFECTION

If you believe you were meant for more—and because you're reading this book, you clearly do—it's time to get out your highlighter. Because as important as it is to follow your inspirations and cultivate decisiveness, there is one more type of action you want to add to your regular repertoire right away; something that all successful people have embraced to get their gifts out into the world, make the difference they know they are meant to make, and get what they're worth.

This is the technique that helps you act on those taps of inspiration and make the decisions that pave the way for transformation. Without this piece of the puzzle, you're much more likely to stay stuck, hidden, and wondering why the universe isn't recognizing and rewarding your value at the highest level.

I'm talking about embracing imperfect action, or what I call "going forward with good enough." If you have any perfection- ist tendencies (and so many of us do), I'm guessing that you are probably shaking in your boots right about now—the thought of not having everything polished and in place can be very scary for a lot of people. As honorable as it is to want to get things just right, the truth is, waiting for things to be perfect is a huge dream killer. We often use perfection as an excuse to not act on our inspirations. We say, "I'll take salsa dancing when I lose 10 pounds," instead of pushing ourselves to go for that thing that's bubbling up in us now.

I have a sister-in-law who has the manuscripts for six novels on her hard drive. Is she afraid they aren't good enough? Does she want to get them all done and then perfect them once more before she releases the first one? I don't know. What I do know is she's certainly not alone—how many book manuscripts never see the light of day because the authors are fiddling with the fonts, changing the tagline one more time, or agonizing over the opening chapter? How many businesses don't get launched because the person who dreamed them up got hung up on figuring out the copy for their website or the color of the logo?

We all have amazing creations and contributions inside us. I know you do too. If you never get those ideas out into the world, the harsh truth is that they will die with you. And then they won't be able to inspire anyone else. It takes courage to share your gifts with the world, whatever they may be. It also takes generosity—because your talents can't help others or make a difference in this world if you never share them.

Maybe you're not a font-fiddler. Maybe you're more concerned with finding the perfect time to do what's calling to you— whether that's when your life slows down, or the market shifts, or the holidays pass. Whatever condition you're hoping for, the truth is that waiting kills possibility. Remember, possibility is a door that stays open only for a short time. If you're convinced you can't get started until your kids are older, for example, or until you have a certain dollar amount saved up, that door could close; and once it does, it's hard to remember why you were so fired up in the first place.

Or maybe you think you need to add to your knowledge, go back to school, or get just one more certification before making a business out of your gifts. While it may be true that you could stand to learn more about your craft, you've already been helping people with your gift even if you haven't been getting paid for that help (yet). Waiting to share it in a bigger way until you've earned another degree means that a lot of people will go without your help, you'll lose a lot of time that could have been spent on building your business, and you'll lose a lot of potential income and on-the-job training. All it really takes to help someone and be seen as an expert is to be a bit farther down the road than the people you're seeking to help. In fact, if you're too far ahead, it can make you less helpful because you can't remember where the people you're trying to help are.

You can keep adding to your knowledge for the rest of your life—and you should—but please hear me when I say this: If the yearning is happening inside you, *you already have enough to get started.* The years of experience you've accumulated and the information and insight that you already have are valuable in their present form. If you're using "getting ready to get ready" as an excuse, you won't get to see how the skills you already have are all that you need to get moving.

> *What you already know is "good enough"*
> *to start helping people in a bigger way.*

The thought of all the novels on all the hard drives, all the trips to Europe that don't get taken, and all the big ideas that don't get acted on breaks my heart. Because the way out—embracing imperfect action—is not nearly as scary as it seems. In fact, it's exhilarating.

THE FREEDOM OF IMPERFECTION

Embracing imperfection is an exercise in the art of letting go. You let go of the need to have everything all figured out before you even take the first step. You let go of your fear—fear of failure, change, or looking like you don't know what you're doing. (The one I battle is the fear of having to do something twice.) Because the truth is, everyone fails, change is inevitable, and every last one of us has many moments of not knowing what we're doing. These things you're trying so hard to prevent are unavoidable.

I know you want to put your best foot forward, and it can be scary to do something that maybe you've never done before. I'm not saying to go forward with shoddy work. I also know that what's typically happening while you're still "working on it" is that you're hiding your gifts. And that's a disservice to the people you are meant to help—including you.

There is a level of trust that you need to access—trust that the 25 years you've spent doing this thing that you're great at, or the things you learned when you overcame that big personal challenge, or the skill that comes so naturally to you that is mystifying to other people, is already good enough to help people. You have to trust that even if you use your gifts imperfectly, you will still deliver a transformation. This is your blessing we're talking about. It's not a fluke or an accident. It matters. And you've got to trust yourself enough to make your offer. (We'll talk about how to organize your gift and your offer in the very next chapter, so don't worry too much about how you'll do this just yet—that part is coming!)

THE REAL YOU IS ALL YOU EVER NEED TO BE

You probably hold off from taking imperfect action because you don't want people to judge you if you make any flubs or show any flaws. The irony is that people will love you for your imperfections even more than if you were all polished and buttoned up.

Here's an example: A few years ago, my dad died and left me as the executor of his will. Although for years he had been telling my siblings and me exactly how much he was leaving and who would get what, it turned out his affairs were not in as much order as he had thought. It quickly turned into a big family mess, and as executor, I was at the center of it. It was weighing on me, and I had a big event coming up where I was leading a three-day boot camp for people who were flying in from all over the world. I couldn't stay embroiled in the family fight *and* serve the people who were coming, so I resigned as executor. It was a tough decision for my family to accept. To me the decision was clear—get embroiled in drama or serve the people I was meant to serve.

In the midst of all this, I got inspired to do something positive. In my coaching, I'm always asking people to stretch, to get uncomfortable, and I wanted to do something that was out of my comfort zone at the event so that my experience would be congruent with what I would be teaching and asking of others. When I think about things that make me uncomfortable, singing in public always comes up first. So that's what I decided to do. I remembered that years ago a friend had invited me to attend her graduation from a class that taught you how to sing from the heart instead of worrying about having flawless execution. I looked up that class online and sure enough, the next class was starting that Tuesday, and it would end the week before my live event. I signed up on the spot.

When the event came around, I didn't feel totally ready. But I was ready enough. When the music to the song I was singing—"The Climb" by Miley Cyrus—started playing, my palms were sweating! I was a little afraid the mic might slip out of my hands.

For the first minute—which felt like an hour—I sounded terrible. The audience was in shock, wondering why their business mentor was singing. I kept going, though, pouring my heart into it, and after the shock wore off and I started to get my stride, they stood up and started roaring. With their support I got less tense, and in the last minute of the song I had my rock star moment!

Because I was vulnerable enough to get up there and sing "good enough," my students were inspired to take action for themselves too. We got cards and letters for months from clients telling us about the huge breakthroughs they were having in their lives and in their businesses. Many shared that they had been on the fence until I sang and they could see where my heart truly was; it was just what they needed to say yes to themselves and join me in my mentorship program. Because I was willing to get out there and be vulnerable, they found the courage to go forward with "good enough" too.

I always make an offer at these events for the people who are ready to take the next step and work more closely with me, and that day twice as many people registered on the spot than ever before. Yep—it was a million-dollar song that started off really shaky. If I had been focused on delivering a flawless performance, I never would have switched on that mic.

BUILD THE PLANE AS YOU FLY IT

To take this idea of imperfect action even further and help you get over any fear that may be keeping you from offering your gifts in a bigger way, you must embrace the idea of "building the plane as you fly it."

Building the plane as you fly it means that you don't wait until you have every little detail figured out and nailed down before you get into motion. As soon as you have a basic structure in place—the walls, the wings, the engines, and, of course, the destination—you take off. You can upholster the seat cushions and pick out the snacks you'll offer for your in-flight service later, when you're cruising over the Midwest.

Maybe your big dream is taking a trip to Europe. You've been thinking about it for years, although you've never bought the tickets for it. A way to build that plane while you're flying it is to buy a ticket to a special event in the country you want to visit—a concert, museum exhibit, or class. Once you've got that low-cost commitment in your hand, it will fuel you to find a way to pay for the airfare and book your hotel or Airbnb. Or if, like my sister-in-law, you've got a big chunk of a book manuscript on your hard drive, you can announce a release date or schedule a launch party that will hold you accountable for producing it and getting it out into the world. The point of building the plane as you fly it is to rope yourself in to doing what your inspiration is telling you to do. Once you're in the air, your only choice is to keep going.

Or maybe you have an inspiration to make money with your gift by packaging your knowledge or expertise into a product or program. Building the plane as you fly it means making an offer that you think will help people and that you know you can deliver, even if your website or your class materials aren't created yet. (We'll talk about exactly how to create and then make that offer in Chapters 9 and 10.) If you find that the people you want to help aren't interested . . . good to know! Aren't you glad to get that valuable information before you spend weeks, months, or even years perfecting that offer? Also, when you go forward with "good enough" and make your offer, you get to listen for what they, the people you aim to help, *do* need and want so you can craft your next offer to be more fitting.

Bob Burnham, an alumnus of my mentorship program, shares a story about his dad that really shows the danger of *not* building the plane as you fly it. Bob's dad was an inventor, and one of his early inventions was a dial-a-line copy holder. Back when typewriters were the norm and there were no scanners, if you wanted to re-create a document, you had to retype it. The copy holder would hold the original document and a dial would move a marker down to the next line of text so that you wouldn't lose your place and potentially make a mistake and have to start again. It sounds like a great idea for the time, but it took so long to develop the prototype and get the patents that by the time Bob's dad tried to sell the copy holder, technology had advanced and no one wanted it. This happened with multiple products; in over 10 years of developing new products, Bob's dad never had a hit.

When I taught Bob about building the plane as you fly it, he got it right away. You see, Bob has a publishing company that helps professionals advance their careers by publishing books. When we first started working together, he regularly gave presentations to groups of professionals who wanted to know how to write a book. Together we hatched a plan for him to create his first product—a series of training videos that outlined the book-writing process. "At one of my lectures, I offered the series of videos that didn't exist yet," Bob recalls. "Four people bought it. I had my next lecture videotaped, and that became my product."

I launched my business in a similar way, even before I knew exactly what I offered or how I would deliver it. After I was fired from my dream job, I was trying to figure out what I was going to do next. I already shared the story of how I hired a coach and he helped me see that I had a natural talent and long track record of closing a really high percentage of sales when I gave educational presentations (we now call this Speak-to-Sell). At first, I had no idea what to do with this insight. How could I turn that knowledge that came so naturally to me into a business? My coach told me to pick my own brain and write down all the things I had been successfully doing without thinking about it. (We'll talk about how you can pick your own brain in the next section of the book.) I wrote down every step I'd take, how I organized my thinking, how I structured my offers, and how I positioned myself. I basically did a big brain dump.

I was still in the process of writing it all down when I was asked to do my first presentation to a small group of women entrepreneurs. I didn't say, "No, I'm sorry, call me again in a few months when I've got everything figured out a little more." I said yes. And I presented the pieces I had already distilled, even though there was still a lot more for me to unpack. At the end of my presentation, I told the women in the audience that I would be putting the rest of my approach in an e-book that would be ready in 90 days. They were so excited that they were practically throwing $97 at me for the e-book that hadn't even been written yet!

Not only did the experience earn me a few thousand dollars, I also got amazing proof that I had something that people wanted. It inspired me to write that book faster and invest a little money to have someone format it instead of doing it myself because people had preordered. That half-built plane is still making thousands of dollars a month for my company, and it contains the core of our Speak-to-Sell philosophy that produces millions of dollars a year for my company.

I'll be teaching you more of the structures that will help you pick your own brain, package your gift into specific products, and make irresistible offers in the next section. Right now, I want you to start observing the ways in which you hold yourself back from action until you feel like everything is perfect. It's time to challenge yourself to step out, be a bit vulnerable, and do the things that are calling to you—imperfectly.

GET UNCOMFORTABLE

Going forward with "good enough" can be uncomfortable. Getting your work out into the world can make you feel super vulnerable. When you get to the point where you're making your offer, you're risking rejection in a big way.

At first, that drive to move through the discomfort will have to come from inside you. You'll have to tap into your courage—which comes from your heart—and step out into the unknown. While your heart will lead the way, you can also get your head on board by looking back on how you have moved through discomfort in the past.

It was uncomfortable for me to go to New York City and pitch this book. I'm used to teaching people who are already established as coaches or service professionals. Speaking one-on-one in an office was unfamiliar territory for me. As I began to prepare for my meetings, I realized that everything I teach about speaking and making presentations applied here too, and it steadied me (and clearly helped me create a favorable impression).

If you look back on your biggest breakthroughs, you'll see that they were not very comfortable—and maybe even downright unpleasant—at first. Maybe you decided last minute to go on a weekend adventure and you had to do all kinds of things to make it happen. Or before you gave the talk that really established you as a thought leader, you had a huge case of butterflies that made you want to run out the back door. Despite the discomfort, you went through with it, and as a result you got to experience something wonderful.

If you encounter moments of fear, resistance, or overwhelm as you consider your next move, remind yourself how great it feels once you get to the other side of that discomfort. That's a piece we often don't consider, because we're too focused on the discomfort we're feeling in the moment.

I can assure you, using your gifts to help others reach for their version of more is the greatest high there is. Once you experience it, you will be so glad you stretched yourself and got uncomfortable. I'll bet that you'll even start to seek out new ways to get uncomfortable so that you can experience more breakthroughs!

While the feeling of discomfort never truly goes away, when you are honoring your "meant for more," it does become more familiar and more manageable—dare I say, comfortable.

Remember, it's much more uncomfortable to live with that feeling inside you that you have more to give and never have it fulfilled or expressed. That sensation is truly painful, and it doesn't go away without experiencing the fleeting discomfort that comes with doing things differently.

Exercise: Determine Your Best Next Move

Getting into imperfect action is all about simply taking the next step, or what I call your "best next move." Focusing on the one step that will make the biggest difference for you *right now, where you are* frees you from having to figure out everything before you get started.

Here's how to determine your best next move:

- Make a big to-do list of everything you need to and would like to do.

- Instead of trying to put that list in order of priority, ask yourself, "What's the one thing I can do from this list that will make the biggest difference, give me the most freedom, or really move the needle for me today?"

- After you've picked that one thing, your best next move, do that thing. Don't go on to identify numbers two, three, and four. Because after that one thing is complete, you will have new capacities. You'll be standing in the new world of having that one needle mover done, and you will see the remaining items on your list differently than the person who had not completed that one important thing.

- Once you've tackled that first needle mover, look at your list again and pick your best next move. Complete it.

- Then, as that new person who has completed two items, look at your list yet again and choose your next best next move. . . .

This is very different than the traditional route of creating a list, ordering it, and then plugging away. The "best next move" strategy honors the confidence and capacity you gain each time you close an open loop.

And once you are moving, imperfect action releases you from the feeling that you have to continually tweak and refine before you can gain momentum.

When you dive in with your first best next move and get it done, you have a new vantage point—it changes your view on what you need to do next to stay in flow.

STEP FOUR

INVITE PURSUIT WITH YOUR IRRESISTIBLE OFFER

Now that you have taken stock of your gifts, assumed the throne, and started taking more action, you are primed to start putting yourself out there and making your offer, and doing it in such a way that it is irresistible to the people who need your help the most.

When you know how to create an irresistible offer, you often won't even have to ask if they'd like what you're offering; they will cut right to the chase and ask, "How can I get started?" I call it "inviting pursuit," and it's exactly what you're going to learn how to do in this step of the Meant for More Formula. Once you have these techniques in your hip pocket, you always know how to craft an offer that makes hearing yes much more likely—and starts the people you were meant to serve down the path of their own transformation.

CHAPTER 9

CLARIFY YOUR OFFER

There's a phrase in the sales world: "A confused mind doesn't buy." A big part of learning how to sell without being sales-y is knowing how to make an offer that is both easy to understand and obviously compelling.

The key to making an offer that is clear and exciting is to start with the end in mind, aka: "reverse engineer." Meaning, you want to give good thought to where you want to take people—the transformation you want them to experience—as well as how you'll get them there—the steps you'll follow. Once you know these two things, you are well on your way to having an offer that your ideal client will thank you for.

A truly irresistible offer has a lot of thought behind it. This chapter is where you will learn how to do that thinking.

Specifically, we're going to cover how to distill the process you use to deliver your gifts, and how to communicate the transformation you offer.

YOU DON'T HAVE TO BE THE BEST EVER
IN ORDER TO HELP PEOPLE

The transformation that you help other people with is probably one that you've created in your own life—whether that's becoming less reactive, learning to be a better parent, getting over postpartum depression, or learning how to manage your money. Even though you've created big changes for yourself in this area, it's likely something you're still in the process of mastering, and it's important to know that that's okay. It's a common pitfall to think you've got to have it all perfect before you can be considered a leader in an area. So please, keep going with the exercises I outline in this section of the book even if you're not feeling like you're in a position to help others because you yourself aren't "finished" yet. All you need to be is a few steps farther down the road than someone else in order to be able to help. In fact, your insight will be more powerful than someone who's had this area all figured out for a long time, because you will be connected to the thought processes and challenges that the people you can help are currently going through. Remember, you've been in the perfect training camp for the work you're meant to do.

UNCOVER YOUR PROCESS

Now let's look a little more deeply at how you've been creating those transformations that you uncovered in Chapter 4 when you looked at your blessing, getting on your dime, or the unique transformation you provide. It may seem like you've been helping people simply by doing what comes naturally to you without a lot of thought or strategy. Yet if you look a little closer, you'll see that every time you've helped someone you've likely followed the same basic process.

I call this process your Unique Branded System, or UBS, for short. You can also call it a formula, blueprint, road map, system, or step-by-step process. You may not think you have one, but if you're helping people get results again and again in a certain area, you likely do. You've been doing it so naturally and effortlessly for so long that you don't even have to think about *how* you help someone—you just do it. I promise you, there is a method to your madness! The system is already there, just waiting for you to see it. It's been hiding in plain sight.

One of the graduates of my mentorship program is a great example of how powerful it is to uncover your UBS. Before she and I met, Diane Halfman was a police officer with the San Diego Police Department, making an hourly wage and living the reality where, if you wanted to make more money, you had to work more hours—in Diane's case, sometimes up to 18 hours a day.

As a police officer, Diane went into thousands of homes. She could see that the homes that had the most drama were also the most cluttered. It led her to study organizing and even run a professional organizing business on the side for over 20 years while also working as a police officer. Through both of her jobs, she noticed that if she could help people shift their environment, it helped them improve their lives in all kinds of ways.

Even in her side hustle, though, Diane thought the only way to grow was to work more hours. When Diane joined my training program, she really drilled down on how she helped people achieve transformation and realized that she had a system—a series of steps that she walked clients through each time she worked with them. By distilling her process into five clear steps (there's something magical about the number five—any fewer steps feels too light, and any more can feel like too much to remember or work through), Diane saved hours of time repeating the same information over and over again to her clients. She also made it simpler for them to understand her teachings, which helped them implement her suggestions that much faster.

Once she had uncovered her process, Diane created an online course that teaches those five steps, which has enabled her to work with clients all over the world. And when she does work one-on-one with clients (who, she likes to point out, will fly her in to see them even if they don't live in San Diego), she can give them access to the online course so that when they are in the same room together they can go straight into implementing the system instead of her having to explain it.

"Having my process mapped out actually make clients feel more comfortable, because they know I've got a proven system," Diane says. "I'm not winging it. This isn't my first rodeo. I've done this work over and over again, and having this process also means that my clients will get predictable results. It's a total win-win."

Now, instead of charging $50 an hour for her professional organizing services, Diane charges $1,997 for her online course and has one-on-one packages that go as high as $15,000. She's working fewer hours and making more money than she ever has, doing what she's great at. And she's able to serve more people because she is not working one-on-one with each and every client repeating the same thing over and over. And *that* is the true power of uncovering your UBS.

To uncover your unique system, you just need to distinguish the way you consistently create transformations for people, whether it's by asking certain questions, teaching certain skills, or outlining the same specific steps. (Don't worry, I've got a system to help you figure out your system! It's coming in just a couple paragraphs.)

The truth is, you don't have to create your Unique Branded System—it already exists.

When you can take a step back and see that you have a proven path to get people to the transformation that only you provide, you'll trust yourself and your knowledge. It makes your gift tangible, and that gives you the confidence to actually open your mouth and make your offer. It also gives the people you can help confidence that you can actually deliver the transformation you're promising them, because they can see that you have outlined the steps it takes to get there. It helps them stretch and say yes to your offer, because they will trust that you can get them to that destination—after all, you have a system.

Distilling your system also helps you work with many people at a time instead of being limited to only working with people one-on-one, so that you can serve more people in less time and generate more income!

I'm not the only one who's a fan of compiling your work into a repeatable system—so was Napoleon Hill, the author of the self-help classic *Think and Grow Rich*. In that book, he wrote:

"General knowledge, no matter how great in quantity or variety it may be, is of but little use in the accumulation of money. Knowledge will not attract money, unless it is organized . . . and intelligently directed, through practical plans of action."

Let's get your knowledge organized so that you can start attracting money with it, shall we?

Exercise: D.A.N.C.E. Your Way to Your UBS

I'm such a fan of systems that I created a minisystem to help you distill and name your own Unique Branded System (UBS). I call it D.A.N.C.E., because it helps you dance your way into the spotlight and perhaps even a new revenue stream!

The **D** stands for "Discover your process." That may sound easier said than done, but all you need to do to get started is grab a set of sticky notes and write down your answers to the following questions:

- What are the steps I take to get results with my friend, clients, or even myself?

- What things do I hear myself saying over and over to people?

Each step you think of goes on a separate sticky note until you have a full wall! Once you've captured everything that you do or say to help people, start to group those sticky notes into categories.

Next, the **A** stands for "Aim to identify the steps." I generally advise that you look to group all your teachings into five steps—it feels like a hefty amount of content without feeling overwhelming.

While you're organizing your steps into groups, **N**otice which ones must be done one-on-one and which ones you can teach to a group, whether in a real-world class; an audio, video, or group call; or a video hangout.

Once you know your steps and how you'll teach them, the **C** in dance stands for "Create hooky labels." It's important that your steps be something clients can remember and that resonates with them. If an acronym works, that's a win too. For example, Diane offers her clients the five-step RESET System (Remove, Evaluate, Systemize, Experience, and Track).

Finally, the **E** stands for "Enjoy the rewards." And, my friend, identifying and then sharing your UBS has too many benefits to ignore. It allows you to leverage your time, make more money than you'd likely ever be able to make if you worked with people one-on-one, help more people, and help people more deeply than if you were working with only one person at a time. You get to dive more deeply into your work with someone who already understands your system than with someone you have to teach as you go. And all it takes is a little focused awareness on what you've already been doing all along.

Perhaps best of all, once you know your process, you can trust yourself to create transformations for people over and over again.

As excited as I am for you to get out on the D.A.N.C.E. floor and experience the opportunities ready to salsa, samba, or boogie with you, just know this: you don't have to have all the steps of your UBS completely written out with accompanying worksheets before you make your offer. You just need to have an awareness of what your system is. Remember, you can build the plane as you're flying it.

COMMUNICATE THE MAIN DISH OF YOUR OFFER

Once you're clear on the transformation you provide and the basic steps of how you deliver that transformation, it's time to find the exact words that you'll use to articulate your offer in such a way that it starts drawing the exact people you can help most toward you. Sounds pretty good, right?

There are three key components to making your offer truly irresistible, and right now, we're going to focus on the first one, the heart of your offer, or what I call your main dish.

When you look at a restaurant menu, there are main dishes, side dishes, and dessert. The transformation you provide is the main dish of your offer; it is the steak. (We will talk about how to add enticing bonuses to your offer—the equivalent of the creamed spinach and the chocolate mousse—in the next chapter.)

To get clear on the transformation you offer, I'm going to walk you through what I call the Unique Offer Identifier. I do this exercise every time I launch a new program. I've also taught it to thousands of clients, and I promise you, it works. It not only helps you communicate your offer, it also helps you value the transformation that you provide, which helps you charge what you're worth.

Exercise: The Unique Offer Identifier

Just one note before we get started: understanding the Unique Offer Identifier is similar to the work you did in Chapter 3 to calculate your ripple and Chapter 4 to uncover your blessing—specifically when you thought about the people you've helped and listed the outcomes and benefits they got from working with you. There is one fundamental twist, however. In this exercise, I want you to really zero in on *one* specific person you've helped who got amazing results from your advice, coaching, or service. This person may or may not be one of the people you thought of in those earlier exercises.

Step 1: Choose one person who got such amazing results from your help that boy, if you could help 100 or 1,000 people in that same way, and maybe even be paid for it, your life would be super fulfilled! (If you can't think of someone you've helped in this way, think instead of a major obstacle in your own life that you have faced and use yourself for this exercise.)

I know it may be hard to choose just one person if you've helped lots of different people with lots of different things. Do it anyway. There's a basic theme to the transformation you provide—an umbrella that all the specific things you do fit under. One of my clients was a leadership coach and a feng shui expert—two very different skill sets. Yet when she sat down to look at the results that her biggest success story in each of these disciplines enjoyed, in both instances, it was accelerated results; the benefit was the same no matter what type of specific counsel she was giving.

Once you've chosen your person, write down their first name so that you don't get tempted to start thinking about a composite of people. You really want to get inside this person's head and think the same way that they think.

Step 2: Answer the following four questions, challenging yourself to get into the head of that person you helped and channel the words *that they themselves would use to describe the results they got.* This isn't the time to use a lot of jargon and marketing speak or worry about sounding catchy, smart, or buttoned up. The more you can describe their results and benefits in real, authentic language, the more compelling your offer will be. On the flip side, the more you try to "get it right," the worse it will go. You really want to embrace imperfection here and not overthink. You're just doing a big brain dump at this point—no one will ever see this work and there are no grades. Just let it flow. Ready?

- **Question number one:** What specific results did this person get from working with you? Write down the exact results: She lost 12 pounds, found a perfect life partner, made $8,000 in a week, rekindled her romance. Go ahead and take credit for the benefits she received; now's not the time to be shy!

- **Question number two:** What additional transformation did she experience because of those results? These are the secondary benefits—maybe she got called for a role in a commercial, landed a dream client, or felt like she and her husband were on the same team again. Really paint the picture here, capturing as many words as you can. Fill up a page and a half.

- **Question number three:** What do you imagine would have been the cost to this person had she not accepted your offer? This one is super important, so don't skip it! You're really going to have to make some assumptions here, because it's all conjecture. That's okay. Would she be divorced by now? Would she have health problems? Would she have amassed more debt? If so, how much? Choose your answers based on the direction the person was headed when they came to you. Remember: no one else is going to read this. You're not going to be fact-checked. This is about understanding the importance of your gifts, not for-tune-telling.

- **Question number four:** What was the biggest source of pain that this person was longing to solve? Was she tired of starting over and over and over with her weight loss? Was she worried about losing her house or getting a scary health diagnosis? Investing time in a dead-end relationship? This is something she may not have ever said to you—or out loud to anyone. It's the kind of thing that maybe she only thought to herself in the middle of the night, so again, you will have to make some assumptions, but take an educat-ed guess. Be bold.

Step 3: Once you have your list of benefits that are described in authentic language, you can use them to form the description of what you do. Take those same plain-English words and add "I help people" before them; for example: "I help people lose a ton of weight in a way that's a lot easier than they think it will be so they can feel sexy again." Write down three to five versions of what exactly it is that you do. Play around with them and run them past people you trust (and people you've just met, say, at a networking event). And then at some point, stop futzing and pick the one that rolls off your tongue the easiest and makes people's eyes light up in recognition. Voilà— that is your unique offer.

HOW YOU DESCRIBE WHAT YOU DO MATTERS

Talking about your work using words that the people who need your help actually use is the first step in making your offer irresistible, so please, don't skip the Unique Offer Identifier exercise! When you find those everyday, non-marketing-speak words, you make it possible for someone to hear what you do and immediately think, "Ooh! I need that! How did she know that's exactly what I'm looking for?" When those folks realize that you can help them with something they really want but haven't been able to find, much less articulate, they will start leaning in to hear more of what you have to say. It's like blowing a dog whistle with the perfect pitch that makes the people you can help the most come running. And that is gold!

As an added bonus, once you know how to talk about your offer in this way, you can use these same phrases in any situation—at a networking meeting, in your website copy, on the back of your business card, during a talk, or when you're being interviewed on a podcast. Doing this thinking now means you no longer have to constantly struggle to express what you do. You find the words that perfectly capture the outcome or transformation that you provide. And by putting "I help people" in front of them, *that's* how you answer the dreaded question, "And what do you do?"

ROUNDING OUT YOUR MAIN DISH

Your main dish is actually made up of two parts—the transformation you provide, and how that transformation is provided. Whenever you're making your offer, whether it's to a family member, a potential client, or your partner, you'll be more persuasive and effective when you focus 90 percent of your energy and words on talking about the difference your offer would make, and only 10 percent on how you're going to deliver it—whether that's the number of face-to-face sessions, group meetings, audio recordings, a Facebook group, or what have you.

Most people get this backward and spend most of their energy talking about the specifics of how their coaching will work, when the class will meet, or how many worksheets are included. The fact is, people don't care nearly as much about these details as they do about the changes they're going to make and benefits they're going to enjoy.

It's like when you're going on vacation—you get excited thinking about being relaxed on the beach in Hawaii, and not about what model of plane you're going to take to get there.

Remember:

> *When it comes to your irresistible offer,*
> *they're buying the destination, not the plane.*

If you really want to help a girlfriend who's suffering in her relationship, and you want to start by going on a walk with her and helping her sort her feelings out, you want to talk to her primarily about how great she'll feel once she gets out, breathes fresh air, and has a new sense of clarity, and not so much about where you're going to walk, how long the walk will be, and what the weather will be like. When you connect to the outcome you want from taking the walk, you'll both find a way to make it work. If it's just about finding a date and picking a place, it will get kicked down to the bottom of your to-do list and may never happen. This is exactly why "let's do lunch" doesn't work—it's about the lunch, not the inspiring outcome of the time you'll spend together. If you both know you want to get together to figure out how to raise money for the new school library and you're connected to the difference that will make for your children this year, it will happen. Whether you're making an offer for someone to formally invest in your product or service, or simply offering to help out a friend, stop selling the plane.

Remember, if you never make an offer, you diminish your power and your opportunities to help other people, and that frustrated feeling that got you to pick up this book in the first place will never go away. That's not what I want for you, and I know that's not what you want for yourself either. All it takes to start getting comfortable with making offers is knowing the structures to use to make them irresistible. Once you know them and start using them, you'll actually *look forward* to making offers. Yes, it's true—you'll relish the chance to make your invitation! So let's continue on to Chapter 10 and the other two components of making an irresistible offer.

CHAPTER 10

MAKE YOUR OFFER IRRESISTIBLE

Irresistible offers are one of my favorite subjects because I love teaching mission-driven, bighearted people like you how to use your gifts to empower other people to make more of themselves. And truth be told, I don't see learning to make these irresistible offers as a nice-to-have kind of thing. I think it's an absolutely vital skill that can transform your world. Because when you learn how to make irresistible offers, you own your gifts and share them, and that's when your life starts to fill up with more—more impact, more fulfillment, more connection, more freedom, and more abundance. And best of all? You help others reach for their "meant for more" too.

Not only is it a disservice not to make an offer, it's a disservice not to make it irresistible. Remember, possibility is a door that only stays open so long. No matter how great the service or product you're offering is, you need to have a reason for the person you're offering it to to say yes *today*. Otherwise the door will close again. People who take time to "think about it" rarely ever come back to say yes later—even if they were super inspired when they heard your offer. The times I have decided to think about accepting someone's offer, I simply went back to my life, where the priorities of being a mother and businesswoman became more immediate than tracking someone down for something that, once the initial excitement had passed, felt like just another thing to fit into my schedule.

This is a crucial point: People usually don't come back after "thinking about it"—no matter how great your offer is. So if you truly want to help people, it's part of your job to help inspire folks to say yes to themselves *on the spot,* while the door of possibility is open and they have a chance to say yes to really making a change.

THE POWER OF BEING PURSUED

When you make your offer irresistible, you invite pursuit. Meaning, your offer becomes like a tractor beam for just the right people who will value it the most and get the most value from it. The irony is, when you learn how to invite pursuit, you almost don't even need to know how to sell! Your people will want to buy from you just because your offer is so compelling; it's almost like they do an internal sales job on themselves.

The reason you don't want to be chasing after people is simple—when you are pursuing someone, you are leaning in toward them. Think of Wile E. Coyote running after the Road Runner; he's leaning forward so far he's almost horizontal. When you are pursuing someone, the other person has only two options—to resist or to submit. Neither of those options is desirable. If they resist what you're offering, they won't take it in and you'll essentially waste your time and scatter your gift. If they submit, they may say yes in the moment and then quit the next day.

> *Someone being pursued cannot pursue;*
> *there's just no space for it.*

Either way, the door of possibility stays shut. In order for them to have the option to pursue you or your work, you have to make an invitation and leave enough space to allow them to step forward. When you do, you are essentially leaning back and inviting the other person to pursue your offer and the gifts, advice, or service that would rock their world.

Think back to the story of Miss Julie and her summer chorus program from Chapter 1. If she had only remembered to get some sign-up forms together and remind the parents to fill out those forms before they left that morning (and sweetened the deal by offering a bonus and a limiter), she would have had parents flocking to her with their filled-out forms. *They* would have been pursuing *her.* Instead, she set herself up to spend the next few weeks chasing down the parents with phone calls, e-mails, and texts, reminding them to sign up for the class. She put herself in the position of pursuer, which not only wastes her time, it feels icky and will likely result in fewer kids in her summer program. Which one do you want to be—the pursuer or the pursued? I'm guessing it's the latter.

Irresistible offers leave room for clients to move forward and follow their desire to grow, learn, and excel. It puts them in the driver's seat, which is empowering. It also allows you to remain the trusted advisor who is there to bless them with your service or expertise should they decide to pursue an opportunity with you—not the pushy salesperson who is trying to get them to part with their money.

YOUR TWO PRIMARY TOOLS FOR INVITING PURSUIT: BONUSES AND LIMITERS

To show you how you can start making irresistible offers in your own life, I'll use an example of one that I regularly make to my kids.

Remember, the main dish is the primary thing that the person you're talking to wants. With my kids, they want to be able to watch their favorite TV show at night with me before we go to bed. So my main dish is the chance to watch an episode of *Modern Family*.

I tell them, "Hey kids, want to watch *our show* tonight?" I'm sure you can guess what their answer is!

From there, I add on the other two ingredients of an irresistible offer: a bonus and a limiter.

BONUSES

If the main dish of your offer is a steak, as we discussed in Chapter 9, the bonus is the dessert—it makes the possibility even sweeter. To make the bonus really enticing, you want to make it something that the person who is going through the transformation that your main dish offers would naturally want. For my kids, the bonus is, "If we get started early enough, we'll have time to watch two episodes." (They're only 20 minutes on Amazon!)

People like to feel they're getting something extra, and giving them a bonus for saying yes often leads them to say to themselves, *Why not do it?* Just be careful not to offer a bonus that requires you to do a lot more work, or else it will feel more like a burden than a bonus to you and the other person will sense your lack of excitement. The best bonuses have a high perceived value for the receiver and cost little for you to provide.

If your offer is related to your business, your bonus may be some additional training, a one-on-one call, or maybe something that you've taught before and recorded that they can benefit from. It's nice to find things that you have already created to offer as a bonus—a spreadsheet you use, a list of resources, some samples of things that have worked for you that they can deploy. Some of your most valuable bonuses are "lying around the shop" if you will. If your bonus requires a lot of time, money, or energy for you to deliver, you won't feel excited about it and it won't be as powerful.

Here's the million-dollar tip. Say you're crafting an offer and you can't find anything to offer as a bonus. Instead of getting wrapped up in a whole new project of creating a bonus, look in your main dish offering for something that is already in there that is really hook-y and really cool and that your clients would highly value if you featured it a bit more; then pull it out and make that the bonus. (In my example with my kids, I'm not throwing a piece of their favorite candy into the deal; I'm merely offering a little bit more of what they're already getting—some TV chill time and snuggle time with me!)

In my own business, when I was first crafting my offer to teach people my system for creating their own irresistible offers, I knew that something they really wanted in addition to the information on how to craft a hot offer were the sample order forms I used to register people into my group programs. So rather than hide those forms in the main dish where they wouldn't be appreciated, I took them out and made them a bonus. I gave away the actual editable PowerPoint file so my students didn't have to go get their forms made by a designer. And I created a simple audio file to talk about how to customize the form to suit their needs. It was only a tiny bit more work on my part and it brought attention to something that people really wanted. Voilà! Everyone wins!

An important thing about bonuses is that they need to be relevant to your main dish. Ask yourself, *What is someone who is investing in my main dish naturally going to want?* When you add a whole lot of bonuses that aren't tightly related, people think: What's wrong with the main dish? You really only need one or two bonuses that are closely related to the main dish and bam— your people will not only love you, they will buy from you too.

LIMITERS

As enticing as a bonus can be, it alone won't light a fire under anyone to say yes in the moment. That role is played by what I call the limiter. Adding a limiter along with your bonus or discount is what makes the magic happen. Limiters create a good kind of tension that can be just the thing that gets someone out of analyzing and into action.

With my kids, the limiter I use is time. I say, "Bedtime is 9:30 no matter when we get started, so the sooner you get ready, the more you can watch. Ready means all papers out of backpacks and anything that needs to be signed by me on my desk, no clothes on the floor, teeth shiny white, pajamas on, phones docked in the overnight charging station in the kitchen—we can't skimp on getting ready just so you can watch a show." They really get busy getting ready for bed when I say this, and the beautiful thing is I don't have to push them or nudge them! When the offer is truly irresistible, people get into action, and they decide to take that action all on their own. In the case of bedtime, I get to read quietly for twenty minutes while the kids hustle to get themselves ready for bed.

Quantity is another great limiter. If you're wanting to help a friend organize her closet, which is something you're great at and she's not, and she's being kinda wishy-washy about scheduling some real time to get it done, you can use a quantity limiter by sharing that you've only got three hour-long slots available in your crazy busy schedule over the next two weeks and ask which one works best for her. That one actually combines time and quantity.

Maybe you would like to test-drive your UBS by offering a small group coaching program to a handful of clients. So you invite a group of friends over to your house to walk them through one step of your three- or five- or seven-step process; and then you make an offer at the end for anyone who wants to take it further to join you in your brand-new program where you'll go through all the steps and cover everything they need to get the transformation that you offer. You might say, "Because we are friends and you've invested your time in being here, you can join for half-price if you sign up tonight." Using a limiter in this way can help the people who are attracted to your offer get off the fence and into action.

I use both time and quantity limiters when I'm speaking on a live stage. I have a special price and some bonuses for people who invest in my training and coaching programs that are available for "this break only" or "today only." Once I walk out the door, the special pricing and bonuses are gone. That's my time limiter. The quantity limiter is something extra just for the first X number of people to get them really popping out of their seats and to acknowledge the action takers—the people who know in their gut that they are ready to invest in themselves and work with me. Both of these limiters help those people who are ready to say yes follow their inner knowing and get into action.

As you're thinking about your offer and deciding what the main dish, bonus, and limiter will be, I recommend keeping the phrase "Do I love it?" top of mind. Because when you feel excited by and connected to your offer, people will be able to sense it, and they will want some of that energy for themselves. On the other hand, if some part of you *isn't* excited about delivering your offer—you really don't want to spend an hour helping your friend organize her closet or deliver your UBS in a small group setting—you will be hesitant when you make it, and people will be able to sense that too.

> **Your irresistible offer also needs to be irresistible to you!**

GET COMFORTABLE WITH TENSION AND AVOID PRESSURE

When you make an irresistible offer to help someone else make change, you will likely be able to feel the tension rise within them as they weigh their options. While I know a lot of people are uncomfortable with tension, you actually *want* to create just enough of it.

Nearly every time someone says yes to transformation, there is tension. It's part of the process. If we never got uncomfortable, we would likely never grow and change. Allowing that tension to rise inside them—which is what using bonuses and limiters can do—is actually a generous thing to do, because it gives someone the space to see where they are, where they want to be, and the gap in between those two things. That's when they flip their own switch and say yes to themselves instead of overthinking things, talking themselves out of it, or worse—convincing themselves that they have to ask permission from someone else.

I'm not the only one who's a fan of creating tension in order to facilitate growth. In his "Letter from a Birmingham Jail," Martin Luther King, Jr., had this to say about it: "I must confess that I am not afraid of the word 'tension' . . . there is a type of constructive, nonviolent tension which is necessary for growth."

So you see, tension isn't just a tool to facilitate the "selling" process. It's a fundamental driver of progress for all of humankind. By getting comfortable with tension—both creating it and allowing it to exist long enough for some kind of shift to happen—you become an agent of change and a servant of progress. As King points out, nonviolent tension is *constructive*. We each can use it to help build a better world.

I know that those of you who are natural-born peacekeepers may be especially uncomfortable with the idea of creating tension. I hope knowing that even someone as devoted to nonviolence as King also believes in tension's power to foster much-needed change will help empower you to embrace it. We all sometimes need a nudge to do what we know contributes to the greater good, am I right? Tension can provide that nudge.

I want to be clear that tension is totally different from pressure. Tension arises on the inside. It's a good thing. Pressure is from the outside, and it can be paralyzing. You don't want to paralyze anyone by pushing or nudging—in fact, you want to inspire them to action. A lot of people mistake the feeling of tension for pressure. So when you make your offer, you may sense the tension it creates and be tempted to backpedal, saying something like "you can think about it" just to relieve the tension. That's actually a disservice.

Nothing kills possibility more than indecision. If you give someone a chance to think about your offer, you are essentially suggesting that they stay undecided. We'll talk about how not to get *attached* to whether someone says yes or no to your offer in the next chapter. For now, remember this: tension is good.

It moves people into action and helps them make a decision. And all transformation is preceded by a decision. So don't tame the tension. Be present and enjoy the beauty of watching the caterpillar evolve. Yes, they have to struggle a bit to work their way out the cocoon. But a beautiful butterfly will soon take flight if you make your offer and create the space for their growth.

Putting All the Pieces Together

Let me give you an example of how the main dish, bonus, and limiters work together in a business setting.

One of my clients, a doctor in private practice, was hosting a series of events at his office designed to introduce his clients—mostly women and, since this was in Los Angeles, many connected to Hollywood—to cosmetic laser treatments. These were upscale evenings with appetizers and cocktails, and every guest received a valuable education and a lovely evening out whether they bought anything or not.

This client hired me to make these events more profitable. At the event, I was happy to see an impressive turnout and a presentation that was well delivered and packed with information. Nothing to tweak there! The problem became obvious when he got to the end of his presentation: there was no "tonight only" limiter.

He did offer a couple of discounts and a few package deals, but they weren't presented as "tonight only." There weren't any pens or registration forms handed out to interested attendees so they didn't have the physical tools to take action. And because he didn't want to appear pushy or sales-y, he simply listed the offerings and left it at that. On a bold day, he'd tell them they had a week to get the special pricing he outlines. As you can imagine, that made no difference in growing his business. This is far too common.

After the event, I went in and restructured his offer so that the customer would get a significant discount if they purchased one of the three special packages within a week of the event. And anyone who purchased the night of the event also received an $1,800 laser hair removal service—quicker decisions meant bigger bonuses.

By doing it this way, the owner didn't have to pressure his guests; they felt some inner tension as they considered whether it was worth trading a night to "sleep on it" for the $1,800 laser hair removal series they would get free for signing up for the nonsurgical laser facelift that night. As you can imagine, this bonus and the limiter of signing up that night was just enough to turn the event from one that felt good yet produced dismal results, into an evening where a majority of the women in attendance signed up that night for their nonsurgical facelift plus free bonus laser hair removal. (I know, I know . . . you're wondering where to get that deal today!)

The point is that with a tightly related bonus and limiter, and the right irresistible offer, the clients did the "sales job" on themselves, leaving the doctor to remain calm and easygoing. Instead of selling, he could be of service, helping attendees figure out which package was right for them so they could purchase on the spot and enjoy a great deal.

The conversion results at these events went through the roof, averaging a 60 percent close rate for packages costing a few thousand dollars each. Needless to say, the owner was extremely pleased.

Once you understand how to craft your own irresistible offers, you will be able to bring people to clarity and help them decide whether they are ready to move along the path toward their version of "more." Best of all, they will never feel as if you've pushed them in any given direction—the people you're seeking to serve remain responsible for their transformation; you are just the catalyst and the conduit. And once they say yes to themselves, they'll thank you for all you did to help them transform their lives!

Now you know the main ingredients of an irresistible offer that will help you invite pursuit, make a big difference with your gifts and talents, and make big money doing it if you so choose. You've got what you need to go out and start making a difference with your gifts—that's how powerful the main dish, bonus, and limiter are. There are a few more strategies you can use to deliver your irresistible offer so that you never veer into pushy or sales-y territory, which we'll cover in the next chapter. Add these to your toolbox, and you'll be ready to make your irresistible offer with ease in any situation.

CHAPTER 11

POSITION YOURSELF AND YOUR OFFER

So now you know the big secrets behind my formula for creating an irresistible offer. You know how to figure out what your main dish is and how to find the words to describe it so that "your" people are compelled to lean in. And you know the secret weapons of bonuses and limiters to help those people make a decision on the spot. You've got the primary tools—you could go out and start inviting pursuit with your irresistible offer today (and I hope you have already tried these out, whether in a formal presentation or in a more casual setting, such as inspiring bedtime with your kids).

Now there are a few more techniques I want you to have in your hip pocket, because they *really* set you and your prospective client up for success. The one thing I hear again and again from my clients is that the main reason they resist selling, or even dreaming of having more of an impact, is because they just want to be themselves. They don't want to be pushy, or slick, or phony in any way. And they certainly are not doing what they're doing to be seen as a salesman. And I don't blame them! The positioning tips that I'm about to share with you really do the selling for you. All that's left for you to do is to pour your uniqueness and personality into them. You get to relax, be yourself, and have fun. As an added bonus, they will also help you get more yeses!

One of my training programs for entrepreneurs is called the Sales, Authenticity & Success Business Academy, and these positioning tips are what deliver on the "authenticity" piece of the equation. While I hear all the time from the members of our community that they love learning how to make money doing their thing, the fact that they can do so while simply being themselves is what makes it all the sweeter.

A really cool side benefit of knowing these positioning tips is that they can be used in all kinds of different situations: making presentations, speaking from a stage, having an impromptu conversation at an event, introducing yourself at a networking meeting, or leading a workshop. These techniques are workhorses—they do the heavy lifting for you. They are also flexible. With these in your toolbox, you're always ready and empowered to make an irresistible offer—and that's how you start getting more opportunities to make a difference with your gifts. And that feels *great*. So let's dive in, shall we?

POSITIONING TIP 1: HARNESS THE POWER OF YOUR PERSONAL STORY

Being vulnerable with people is actually a source of power. When you share your personal story, you give people the chance to connect with you on an emotional level. And connecting with others is a basic human need—so being vulnerable helps you be of service to others. The benefits flow to you too, because people are much more likely to buy from, or enter into a deeper relationship with, people they know, like, and trust. Being real is how you facilitate that affection and that trust, which ultimately helps you support others in making meaningful change.

Here's an example: This past Christmas, a friend of mine was sharing with everyone gathered around the table for a holiday meal what a difference meditating has made in her life. Just hearing her story and being in her presence, I could sense a change in her energy, which inspired me to ask her if we could meditate together. We did, and that one session got me back in the habit again.

Many of our clients discovered their "meant for more" by authentically sharing their story and what they overcame. From there, people started to inquire more about their experience, and before they knew it, they were using the systems in this book to dust off that gift, clarify it, and offer it as a service. For example:

- Esther Miller, who was a victim of clergy sexual abuse when she was younger, now helps other victims of sexual abuse self-heal their trauma so they can have a breakthrough instead of a breakdown.

- Brent Martin, who cured himself of Lyme disease, started a consulting business called Lyme Less, Live More to help others do the same.

- Jennifer Patterson, a Massachusetts native and financial planner living in Bermuda, who had to figure out the ins and outs and financial consequences of running a business in a new country, now runs Cross Border Living—a consulting firm that specializes in helping other expats navigate multinational hurdles.

Sharing authentically isn't just talking about how great things are going for you. The friend I talked with at Christmas opened the conversation by saying that her relationship had been suffering and she had not been making good choices. When you are vulnerable with other people, they pay attention. Being real is a key component of being irresistible, and the beautiful thing is, it allows you to stop obsessing over every detail and trying to make things perfect. It allows you to access a feeling of ease and lightness, and that is palpable and attractive to other people who will be relieved to see evidence that they don't have to be all buttoned up in order to be of service.

We all have a lot of stories we can tell. This isn't just about getting personal. It's about sharing the story that reveals why you are inspired to make the offer you're making. What prompted your interest in this topic? What obstacle did you overcome? What unpredictable victory did you have that led you to be making this offer?

> *Make sure any personal story you tell directly relates to the offer you're going to make.*

One word of caution: You need only share a small part of your story to make a point, and you've got to know what that point is. Stories may contain a multitude of points. If you keep your offer in mind and remember that this story is helping your listener understand your passion for making that offer, you won't get sidetracked. This is another place where reverse engineering comes in. You want to ask yourself before you make your offer what your intention is in telling your story. There are many good reasons to share—you want to make sure you know which one you're going for.

POSITIONING TIP 2: SHARE YOUR CREDENTIALS

Some people may find being vulnerable uncomfortable and would rather talk about their education, training, honors, and achievements. Others would much rather talk about their personal story than talk openly about their expertise—it can feel like bragging or like a plea for attention, and that can make them feel really uncomfortable.

While it can be easier to have someone else talk about you, as when you're getting introduced before a speaking engagement, you won't always have that option. If this is the case for you, it can be helpful to get the juices flowing by talking about your qualifications as if you were someone else. I saw the power of this firsthand once when I was visiting Santa Fe, New Mexico, and enjoying browsing the shops along the plaza. When I walked into one gallery, I saw a statue that just spoke to my heart. It was a bronze figure of a woman with her head and arms raised up to the sky, as if she was opening herself up to receive a huge blessing from above. I started chatting with the woman working in the gallery, who excitedly told me all about the artist and the intricate processes she used in her sculptures. I loved hearing every detail of how this openhearted figurine was made and wanted to know more about the person who made her. That's when the woman who was helping me burst into tears and admitted that she herself was the artist, and the sculpture was named Divine Providence.

This artist was uncomfortable talking about her expertise and owning her credibility. She managed to do it by pretending she was talking about someone else. While I don't recommend this as an ongoing practice, it's a great exercise you can use to get in touch with your own credentials and with how truly awesome you really are.

Remember: your gifts are your most valuable offerings. If you don't see them as valuable and worth sharing, no one else will either. If your friend had all the credentials that you had, you wouldn't hesitate to tell other people about them—offer that same generosity and pride to yourself.

To help you get more comfortable with sharing your credentials, take a moment to list them. What are they? They include your degrees and education, but they don't stop there. What awards have you won? Prestigious organizations you're a member of? Leadership positions you've held, whether you were paid for them or not? What have you been doing for 5 years, 10 years, 20 years? Have you authored a book? Remind yourself of all you have accomplished, and it will help you see the value in what you have to offer.

Of course, there is a balance to be struck here. Credibility and vulnerability sit on opposite ends of a teeter-totter—you don't want to rely too heavily on either one or your energy will be out of balance.

If you keep your vulnerability under wraps and only talk about your degrees and accomplishments, it can also feel a little off to the other person. They will secretly wonder what you're hiding. And you can come off a little self-congratulatory.

On the other hand, if you only share your foibles and hardships, or if you share your story but it clearly still upsets you, people will have a hard time gaining confidence and trust in you. That's why it's so important to keep the teeter-totter relatively even.

This shows up for me all the time when I'm speaking. Sometimes the person who is introducing me will say something like, "You're going to love Lisa; she's adorable and so much fun!" That's when I will come on stage and make it a point to mention that I've been named to the *Inc.* 500 list of the fastest-growing privately held companies in the United States two years running and have graduates in 134 countries. And sometimes someone will introduce me with *only* those impressive-sounding accomplishments, and I'll step on stage and say, "And I did it all with two toddlers in tow, moving every two years while my then-husband was working his way through surgical fellowship!" Sharing these personal details helps make me more relatable.

A question I hear a lot is: How do I build credibility if I'm just starting out? Your personal story can also lend you credibility, particularly if there's a particular struggle you've overcome or achievement you've attained—you've been married 25 years, or lost 100 pounds and kept it off, or stayed connected to your kids through their teenage years or, as in my case, built a home-based business because you were moving all the time while your husband was in medical school. The challenges you've faced and victories you've had demonstrate the knowledge, commitment, and insights you've earned, and that also contributes to trust.

Another way is to borrow the credibility that you created in your prior life—if you taught third grade for 15 years and now you're wanting to help people as an organizer, you can talk about how your classroom was always the most conducive to learning because of your attention to organization. Or if you're new to life coaching and you were known for your knack for mentoring your staff when you were a marketing director for a Fortune 500 company, that completely relates.

My point is, you've been in the perfect training camp for the transformation you provide—I know that your credibility is there if you look closely enough. Once you discover it, find concise ways to let others know about it; it will help you create trust.

POSITIONING TIP 3: OFFER SOCIAL PROOF

There's nothing more persuasive than hearing what a third party—who has nothing to gain—has to say about the benefit of whatever it is you're proposing. Humans are social creatures. We care what other people think, and we look to other people for inspiration. That's why case studies and testimonials can go a long way toward building trust and help sell your offer.

Say you're pitching a project at work and you need the boss's approval to get started. After you've established that you've identified a way to solve a problem you've observed, state how either a similar project internally or at another company has delivered results. Or if you're pitching your kids on the prospect of taking piano lessons, mention a conversation you had with one of their friends about how piano was their favorite after-school activity. The only caveat is, *these have to be true*, and they have to come from the heart. You want to share social proof with the intention of helping the person you're "selling" to make a decision. It's even more powerful if you get a quote from someone directly—like when someone endorses you on LinkedIn.

If you're just starting out in your chosen field, you can borrow testimonials about your category, even if you don't yet have personal case studies yet. I had a client who bought a pod storage unit business. Because he was brand new, he didn't yet have any satisfied customers. So he went on the Internet and found all kinds of quotes from people who had used the same type of storage units, raving about how their stuff got less damaged in them and it was more cost-effective and convenient than renting a storage unit in a building. In this case, he borrowed public testimonials for his category, and you can do the same thing. If you're a brand-new life coach, perhaps a celebrity has mentioned in an interview how much coaching has helped them achieve their goals—you can use that quote in your offers.

POSITIONING TIP 4: LET PEOPLE KNOW IN ADVANCE THAT YOU'LL BE MAKING AN OFFER

This is one of my favorite selling secrets that effortlessly creates curiosity in the person you could help and gets them to lean in more closely so they can hear what you're saying. In my business, we call it seeding—planting seeds about what your offer is before you ever make your offer.

The dictionary definition of "seed" is: "A fertilized plant ovule containing an embryo capable of developing a new plant; a source; offspring; to plant seeds in."

In my definition of seeding, you give valuable little tidbits of information to get the person started—how many depends on how much time you have—and you also show them where those super valuable nuggets you just gave came from. You share that if they want more you'll tell them how they can get it before you finish up. You absolutely want to deliver value within your initial conversation. You also don't want to give away the whole store, because then you'd be right back to giving your gifts away for free, which you already know feels terrible because the receiver so often does nothing with them. Also, since the person you're talking to hasn't flipped their own switch and said yes to your offer yet, they wouldn't take your advice to heart—it would go in one ear and out the other.

Seeding is how you let the person know that there's so much more available to them—if they want it. It does the selling for you because it encourages those folks who *do* want more information to make a decision and say yes to themselves.

Seeding is simply letting people know about what you have to offer *before* you officially offer it to them. That way, when you do get to the point where it's time to invite pursuit with an irresistible offer, your audience knows what's coming. They aren't surprised and they—and you—won't feel like you're all of a sudden switching in to "sales mode." You'll simply be telling them about what you've already told them you're going to tell them about. When you seed, there's absolutely no reason to feel bad or sales-y about making an offer. You're just fulfilling a promise! That's typically pretty easy for people to get behind—even if you aren't yet totally comfortable with the idea of making an offer. You don't want to leave your people hanging, do you? So plant those seeds.

There is a particular approach I take with seeding that has been extremely effective over the past 20-plus years of my career. It has certainly been one of the keys to my success as a speaker, trainer, and salesperson. It even worked when I was selling shoes in my late teens!

I worked in a large independent shoe store that had women's, men's, and children's shoes. We had a large selection of sizes and because of that, we attracted women who had a hard time finding the right fit elsewhere. When I encountered one of those women, I would tell them how excited I was to help them find just the right brand, and that once we did, they should get it in every color! Almost every time that was exactly what they did. I would also share that if we had time, I'd be happy to help them with a surprise for their husband or maybe slippers for the whole family for the holidays. They almost always partnered with me to make time. As a result, I was the only salesperson allowed to sell across all three departments. It was not uncommon for me to walk up with a stack of boxes six pairs of shoes high, place them on the counter, and then escort the woman to the men's and sometimes children's department. To this day I still remember my thirteen-pair sale to one super happy woman! The seeding let her know what I had available for her up front and created the desire in her to have it, without being pushy or sales-y.

Here's how I do it in my talks. I tell the people in the audience right from the beginning, "Since we have a limited amount of time together, I'm going to give you everything I can in the time

145

we have. From experience, I can tell you that there will be some topics that you will want to dive deeper into and we just won't have time. So, along the way, I'll show you how you can get more on that subject through one of the resources I offer. And then later today, I'll show you how you can get some amazing deals on my products and services if you feel inspired and want more."

I call this approach "partnership from the start." It relaxes the person you're talking to because they don't have to steady themselves for some big close—you told them what you were going to do, and you've done it in such a way that they are eager to hear more. And it relaxes you too, because you can focus on serving them, not selling them.

Seeding is a super fun skill to learn that can help you sell more products or services, and is just as effective in getting your friends together for a weekend trip. Recently one of my girlfriends wanted to pull together a girls' weekend for six of us to go to Cabo. There are about 15 in our close friendship circle. So all week she shared a bunch of fun stories and posted beautiful pictures from her last trip to Cabo with her husband. By Friday, she tossed out the dates in a group text to all 15 of us and said, "I don't have time to herd cats on this. The travel agent is holding spots for six of us in three weeks. Call him directly and grab them. First come, first served!" And zip. The spots were gone that day. If you were paying close attention, she used a quantity limiter too!

POSITIONING TIP 5: BE COMMITTED BUT NOT ATTACHED

The overarching principle that will make all these positioning tips more effective is your "come from"—the intention that you set before you start a conversation with someone or a group of people you might be able to help. You want to be committed but not attached: committed that they make a yes or no decision but not attached to whether they say yes or no.

When you can let go of feeling like you *have* to get a yes in order to be successful, you get to relax and simply be of service. You know that all the structures you've learned are doing the heavy lifting, and that the only person who needs to do a "sales job" is the person who's hearing your offer—and she needs to sell herself. It also allows you to remain the trusted confidante who is there to bless them with your expertise should they decide to pursue an opportunity with you.

When you are committed but not attached, you make it your goal to give people exactly what they need to make a decision so that they can say yes or no confidently. If they say no, they'll be able to do it with absolute clarity—and clarity itself is a huge gift. Then that person gets the peace of knowing that while, yes, there's an area of their lives that they'd like to be better, it's not a priority for them right now. They can stop feeling like they ought to be doing something differently.

I consider it a disservice to leave people with one more thing called "figure out if I want to do XYZ or not." It's like adding another item on to an already too-long to-do list. I prefer to give them everything they need to make a choice and then move on with their lives in the direction that serves them. Committed but not attached is how you do that without being remotely pushy or sales-y or shy and fearful.

NOW GET OUT THERE AND MAKE SOME OFFERS!

Now that you know all these structures—the three ingredients of an irresistible offer as well as the five positioning tips we covered in this chapter—you have all the tools you need to help people (including you!) move along the path toward their "meant for more."

Just knowing a concept isn't enough to create change. You've got to take action based on these concepts to really integrate them into your life. So for the next three days, come at every conversation that entails putting your ideas forward from a place of partnership; share a bit of your own story and/or your credentials in this area; weave in at least one example of how someone else has benefitted from what you're suggesting; and—if you have enough time and you're sure the person is interested in hearing them—give all the specifics that would help them reach a decision. I think you'll find that implementing these techniques will feel pretty great—they free you up from feeling like you've got to sell the other person, and they keep you focused on serving. And that is such a relief!

Best of all, no one will ever feel as if you've pushed them in any given direction—you'll simply open up a door of possibility and then give them everything they could possibly need to decide whether they want to walk through it or not. The people you're making an offer to retain their autonomy and their agency, which means they'll be more invested in whatever information or advice you're offering. The people you're seeking to serve remain responsible for their transformation—you are just the catalyst and the conduit.

And now, allow me to do a bit of seeding . . . I've created a very successful business around teaching the structures that will help you help more people and make great money while doing it. I've put the foundational principles into this book, but there are more! There are structures that help you create more opportunities to make your offer. There are structures that help you develop your own training programs and packages that serve your people at an even higher level than simply advising them one-on-one. And there are structures to systematize your efforts so you always know what to do next and you get to stop reinventing the wheel. While I've zoomed in on helping you gain the confidence and clarity to make your offer in this book—if you zoom out, there is a lot more to the picture.

For many of you, the next logical step is to learn some structures around being able to make your offer more frequently and with even more confidence so that you can serve more people, and if you so desire, even make money with your unique gifts. At the end of the day, there are only four ways to make your offer: one-on-one (whether in person or on the phone), presentations in live settings or through webinars or podcasts (we call this structure Speak-to-Sell), live events or intimate workshops or retreats, and online platforms (which is the most exciting for many people these days, as you can help people all over the world quickly and with low overhead).

To do a deeper dive into our structures to make your offer in all of these scenarios, visit www.LisaSasevich.com to access my suite of training options. I'll introduce you to the glorious path I've followed to create and grow my business. I have taught thousands of mission-driven entrepreneurs from over 100 countries how to profit from their knowledge in a way that feels good, and you better believe that if learning more from me so that you can live your Meant for More life is your best next move, I'd be happy to make you an irresistible offer.

STEP FIVE

LIVE YOUR MORE

Making your offer, helping more people, and receiving more rewards is a wonderful, thrilling ride. It can expose you to some of your highest highs of your life. Of course, though, those highs wouldn't be possible without some valleys in between. This final step of the Meant for More Formula is about navigating those valleys and spending more of your time in the peaks, enjoying the fresh air and seeing new vistas of possibility. I call it "living in the Himalayas"; it's exhilarating, but it can also take your breath away. Here then are some tools to help you navigate the majestic mountains that you are headed toward with your Meant for More life.

CHAPTER 12

MAKE YOUR QUANTUM LEAP WITH GRACE

Following the Meant for More Formula can upgrade your life in wonderful and important ways, whether it's a deeper sense of fulfillment, higher self-confidence, more money, improved relationships, elevated energy, or some combination of all of the above.

While it's true that acting on your sense that you are meant for more puts you on a path of growth, it is also true that change, even positive change, can be stressful—maybe even a little scary.

It's like you are swinging on a trapeze called your life, and then in the distance you start to notice another trapeze—a bar that is calling you to make a leap and grab it. When it first starts to present itself, you may only be able to see a blurry vision in the distance. You have a sense that if you make the leap, you'll get in touch with a new level of leadership, courage, and vision that you just can't access from the bar you're swinging on now.

And yet, you're also pretty comfortable on that current trapeze. You know exactly how to hold on and at times even enjoy the ride.

What has to happen to get from the trapeze you're currently on to the other one, from where you are to what you see is possible? You have to let go.

And that means you have to fly through the air, untethered, with no safety net beneath you. It could be just a nanosecond, or it could be a few months. That is such a life-changing moment.

I know this moment of being between the trapezes so well. When I was in my 20s, working for big corporations, I was swinging so happily on my trapeze. I was using my gifts. I no longer had to feel the pain of wondering what I was doing with my life. And then came the time to let go. Then in my 30s, I started working in a small, more entrepreneurial company that felt like my dream job and poof, I was nudged off that trapeze and was midair with no new trapeze to grab on to, and that was more than uncomfortable. It was terrifying.

Maybe you have begun to see or feel that trapeze in the distance, or possibly you're already untethered, between the trapezes.

If you actually grab on to the new trapeze without releasing the old one, you can get really stretched, really fast. It feels so uncomfortable. Maybe you're trying to do the same thing you've already been doing *plus* create something else entirely new, and you're overworked and scattered. Or maybe someone you love says something that makes you feel judged, or your self-doubt kicks in and you start to think that the life you're headed for is unsustainable. The truth is, you can only maintain holding on to both for so long. And a lot of times what happens is that you let go of the new thing and go back to the old trapeze, because it all felt too hard or too uncomfortable. When the truth is, you never got to experience the new trapeze; you got stuck on the experience of holding on to both.

Even when you summon your courage and leap for the new trapeze, it's sometimes true that things feel worse before they get better. You may have to end relationships with people who can't support you on this new path. You may have to manage some

154

anxiety-producing financial leaps. Initially, you may not have as much time with your friends or family as you'd hoped. In many cases your old ways of comforting yourself stop working and you have to let go of who you've become and what you've become comfortable with in order to embrace the upleveling that has already begun.

Wherever you are on the trapezes, making big changes can bring up a lot of fear—just like if you were actually swinging on a trapeze and you looked down. It might trigger a wave of panic. Fear of failure and fear of success are both exceedingly common—and oh-so-human—reactions to putting yourself out there in a bigger way. That fear can then trigger resistance, which, just as its name suggests, starts to weigh you down and slow your progress. If you don't recognize resistance for what it is, it can grind you to a halt.

You may not experience any fear or resistance as you claim your "meant for more," but that would be pretty rare. Once you know about resistance, though, you can identify it for what it is and not take it as a sign that you're doing things wrong. Knowing about resistance can help you grab on to the next trapeze more firmly and confidently, which will also help you let go of the old one and fully experience the new possibility that you've stepped into.

THE TWO TYPES OF RESISTANCE

There are two different kinds of resistance you'll want to keep an eye out for. They are:

- **Internal resistance.** This is the voice of your inner critic, who says things like, "You're not ready." "This will never work out." "You never followed through on that other idea and you won't this time either." "The timing isn't right." "You need to handle this other thing first!" We're all vulnerable to self-doubt when we're moving toward our higher calling.

I remember a time when I was preparing to host a big event—a magical three-day training that people were paying good money for and traveling from all over to attend. Although I didn't realize what I was doing at the time, whenever I wanted an excuse not to do the work that needed to be done before the event, I would e-mail my ex about something related to the kids. Those e-mails were actually a subtle form of internal resistance—I was seeking a distraction from the slightly scary thing I had coming up, and boy, did I get it. There was a year in my life when every time I was about to take the stage, I'd get a text or an e-mail from him that said something upsetting. Until I recognized it as my own resistance, it seemed that he just had amazing timing for upsetting me before every big event I had. Once I figured out that I was the one generating it and that it was a form of internal resistance sneaking into my path, it stopped happening. (I also stopped sending those instigating e-mails!)

- **External resistance.** These are the things that happen in your life seemingly out of nowhere. You save up money for your dream trip and then you get a leak in your ceiling and you have to spend that travel money on repairs. Or you've got a big presentation later that day and your kid wakes up sick. One of my early spiritual teachers called this external resistance "the illusion." It shows up when you're on the verge of doing something big and meaningful, and it shakes you and weakens your confidence. Sometimes to the core.

If you know you were meant for more, you've got to get good at identifying resistance and moving forward anyway. That moving forward will require courage. The good news is that it will build more courage that you will be able to draw on anytime you experience resistance in the future—and if you are on a path of growth (and as a reader of this book all the way to almost the end, I can assure you, you are), you will need that reserve. As Price Pritchett wrote in his book *You*[2], "Courage is not the absence of fear and anxiety, it's proceeding in spite of those feelings. So press on."

Whatever form your resistance takes, it's very tempting to take it as a sign that you are on the wrong track. I have come to see resistance as a sign that you're on to something good, and that you're on the right track! And when you're on to something *really* big and juicy, the illusion kicks in harder. If this weren't the case, everyone would be living their blessings and there would be no need for this book.

Now, when I hear my inner critic getting riled up or I experience something weird and out of the blue in my life, I know that whatever I'm working on is truly coming from an inspired place, and I let that knowledge bolster me in going off to take more action. And that's exactly what you want to do in the face of resistance, because when you keep going, your internal guidance system will kick in even stronger.

Here's an anology that may help. Think of yourself like a fancy new sports car—it's impossible to drive when it's in park. As soon as you put it in drive and start moving forward, the power steering kicks in, the GPS starts working, and you start moving toward your destination. Even if you get off track a little, that GPS can recalculate your route *so long as you are moving*. When you can keep moving forward even when the illusion is showing up, everything will shift for you.

Every time you stay the course in the face of resistance you gain strength, confidence, new capabilities, and momentum. You grab on to that new trapeze more strongly.

To help you handle any resistance that may crop up with a minimum of drama and doubt, there are five tools I want to share with you that will help you keep going.

1. Upgrade your circle.

It's not a new theory that you become the sum total of the six people you hang around the most. That's because energy and mind-set are contagious. To really become comfortable in your new life of reaching for your "meant for more," you've got to be very mindful of who you spend time with and transform your circle to include only those who are helping you move forward, not holding you back.

In many cases, the most well-meaning people will be the ones who can act as the biggest drag on your forward momentum—not because they don't want the best for you, but because of their own fear. Some of these people may be in your own family. While I'm not suggesting you cut ties with anyone, I do want you to be conscious of whom you reveal your plans and your progress to. If you've started making your irresistible offers and you're starting to see some results, but you're not entirely confident yet, even one raised eyebrow from your sister or your spouse may send you into a spiral of doubt.

You still need people you can be vulnerable with—a tribe you can share your successes, questions, and fears with. This is why joining a community or group of like-minded people is key—it's simply amazing how inspiring it is to be in close contact with people who are also seeking to bring their "meant for more" to life. This may mean joining a Facebook group of like-minded people, or an in-person version of the same. Just be sure that everyone is dedicated to staying the course in the face of the illusion and in agreement to lovingly provide feedback when you see each other getting gripped by it. We all need a tribe. Make it a priority to find yours. (And if what you're discovering here feels like a fit, my community and I are here for you!)

2. Give yourself permission.

It's so common to feel that you need buy-in from your spouse, partner, or boss before you can really commit to making positive changes for yourself. I hear it again and again from the people who are contemplating investing in our training: "I need to check with my husband first."

I understand the desire to have your partner's blessing, I really do. Just take an honest look at that thought and make sure that the person you really need permission from isn't yourself. What I also have seen over and over again is that when someone acknowledges her sincere desire and gives herself permission to pursue it, everyone around her recognizes it and gets on board.

If you suspect that you are holding back your own approval, revisit all the ways in which sharing your "meant for more" helps other people—the actual people you help, your family, your community, and the world at large. See if getting back in touch with the good you're capable of creating for others helps your Little Me get on board. Sometimes when we remember that it's not really about us, but about creating the highest good for everyone, it helps us make the big leaps.

3. Acknowledge your wins.

When you are on the journey of unwrapping your gifts and sharing them with the world, it's kind of like being an early explorer sailing out to sea—even though you keep sailing, the horizon never appears to get any closer. The only way to truly see how far you've come is to pause and look back at the shore.

You have to acknowledge your own progress on this path because there's no gold star or merit badge waiting for you from your boss, company, or troop leader. No one is going to say, "Great job for taking the time this week to work on your book," or "Congratulations on making an irresistible offer today!"

You can acknowledge your wins by keeping a running list of every little accomplishment you make—either in a notebook or your planner. Commit to writing down at least three wins every day, and then share them with people who care. The more you can do this with like-minded people the better.

The point isn't to brag, although bragging's just fine—it's about claiming the ground you've taken. The beauty of being open about your accomplishments is that it lets people see that you're on a mission, and it sparks inspiration in those who know they are "meant for more" as well.

4. Create structure for yourself.

If you want to see what you're committed to, look at your calendar and your checkbook and/or your monthly credit card statement. The things that you give your time and your money to are your priorities, whether you realize it or not. For example, if you want to save your marriage, you go to therapy—it's in your calendar and it shows up on your bank statement. If you aren't seeing the results you'd like to see on your quest to bring your "more" to life, you probably need to commit some time and money to create structure for yourself, because structure creates freedom. Then you can relax knowing that your "meant for more" is in your calendar and woven into your life.

The best way to give yourself that structure is to commit to something that will keep you on track, accountable, and continuing to learn—an online program, one-on-one coaching, a group mastermind, a weekly class, or a committed accountability buddy. By adding some structure to going after your goals, you are essentially shoving a wedge into that open door of possibility and keeping it open long enough for you to walk through it.

A few years ago when I decided to make myself really uncomfortable by singing at my live event, I didn't just hope it would work out. If I had, I would have ended up worrying for six weeks before panicking and backing down. Instead, I signed up for a six-week class that supported me with structure from the time I made the decision until the time I stepped on that stage. Because I did that, I could rest and stress way less, knowing that I had a structure that would teach me everything I needed to learn in the time I had. I still had to show up to class and rehearse, mind you—structure gives you freedom from worry, not necessarily a free pass from doing the work.

You have to put things in your calendar well in advance; otherwise it's too easy to say you don't have the time. If you plan the times when you'll work on developing your offer and deliver your service in advance, they will magically coexist with all the other things you have going on in your life. You dictate what goes in your calendar; your calendar doesn't dictate what you can and can't do. Sometimes we forget that and get into a mode of consulting our calendar to see what's possible. Remembering that you are the author of your calendar is one of the most powerful breakthroughs you can have!

5. Be a river, not a pond.

In Chapter 3, we covered how focusing on lifting others as you climb can inspire you to start making irresistible offers. And we discussed how powerful it is to practice sharing the rewards of your efforts—if sharing your "meant for more" means you have extra time, then donate your time to the causes and people you care about. And if it creates more income for you, then donate some of that extra money to the people, places, and institutions that feed you spiritually.

As powerful as it is to give when your schedule, bank account, and inspiration allow, if you really want to leap to that next trapeze and never look back, consider making giving a structured part of your life by tithing. I got this idea from a book by Edwene Gains called *The Four Spiritual Laws of Prosperity*—I swear by the wisdom in this book, and often give copies of it to my clients. By her definition, tithing is giving 10 percent of all the money that comes your way to a person, place, or institution that feeds you spiritual food or reminds you of who you are.

If that thought has you quaking in your shoes—*What about paying off my debts? Or saving for retirement?*—just try it as a six-month experiment. I guarantee you'll never go back to keeping everything you earn to yourself, because whatever value you deliver will be greater and more meaningful. You won't want to give up the good feeling it provides and all of the collateral blessings it brings to your life.

In 2008, right after I got fired from my dream job the day before Christmas Eve, I attended a talk by Edwene Gaines in Los Angeles at the Agape International Spiritual Center. That night, I vowed to contribute 10 percent of everything I earned for six months, fully expecting that if it didn't work I would just stop.

At that point in my life, when I was between trapezes, it felt really scary to give away any of the money I brought in. Yet I did it anyway, and I believe it helped me move to the new trapeze much more quickly than if I hadn't been doing it; I got clarity on my gifts really fast and ended up almost tripling my income from that old job within those six months.

Beyond that, tithing made every step I took and reward I earned even sweeter, and my personal abundance just kept skyrocketing too. Ten years later tithing is still at the top of my list of spiritual practices.

It's important to note that tithing isn't necessarily the same as donating to good causes. You want to tithe to people and places because they inspire you, not because they can demonstrate a need. You can absolutely still give to causes, but those donations don't necessarily count as a tithe unless your donation grows the inspiration and doesn't just feed the need. This is an important distinction because what we focus on grows—and we want to grow inspiration, not need.

You can even tithe to individuals. Leave a big tip for the waitress who says something you needed to hear at just the right moment in just the right way. Or pick up the tab for a couple eating at another table at the restaurant who are laughing and loving being in each other's presence, thereby giving you a glimpse of inspiration of how you want your own relationship to be. (Anonymously pay their bill for them and tell the waiter to say, "Your bill has been covered. It's a little gift from God.") In my company, we tithe to our own clients for how inspiring they're being, and my whole team gets in on the monthly act of nominating the ones who are going for it and inspiring us the most!

Tithing is a powerful way to feel that you're truly making a difference. It encourages you to get out there with your biggest heart and your best stuff, which is a surefire way to grow your fulfillment, your impact, and your rewards. When you're in fear and resistance, tithing lifts you up and reminds you of who you are and sends a message to the universe that you are committed to helping others and that you are open to receiving more help from the universe in order to do it. Tithing raises your energy and your frequency, and when you do that, obstacles melt away and you move forward like a hot knife through butter.

LET YOUR FORWARD MOMENTUM CARRY YOU

Some people will spend their lives just looking at that other trapeze or trying to pretend it's not there. Since you're reading this book, I'm guessing that you have a desire to reach for it— and if you've read this far, I'm willing to bet you've built up some pretty significant momentum to carry you forward. You may let out a big yelp as you leap or land a little less gracefully than you would have liked. It doesn't matter if your journey to the next trapeze isn't a perfectly Instagrammable experience. It only matters that you get there—that you stretch out your hand, take a deep breath, and make the leap.

CHAPTER 13

YOUR 30-DAY MEANT FOR MORE CHALLENGE

I trust that by now you have implemented some of the structures I've included in this book, and you've started to get confirmation that what you suspected all along—that you were meant for more—is true. I want to take this opportunity to congratulate you on the work you've done so far, and to encourage you to keep going (and going and going). Because sharing your "more" with the world isn't a one-time proposition.

Although it may morph in its expression over the years, your "meant for more" is part of who you are. It's something you can't keep under wraps for very long because once it gets even the smallest amount of fresh air, it just keeps growing and growing and growing; and that's a good thing!

I have been passionate about helping people make their offer for a long time—as I'm writing this, it has been my primary business for 10 years, but it started long before that; I don't remember a time when I wasn't interested in helping people say yes to themselves. And I am still peeling back the layers of my gift. I bet I have only downloaded about 30 percent of what I know about making irresistible offers—despite having spent the past decade doing it in a focused way. Living into my idea that I was meant for more has been and continues to be a process of discovery for me, one that keeps leading me to new opportunities and insights.

The more you get out there and implement the strategies contained within the Meant for More Formula, the more opportunities you'll have to understand the transformation that you provide in a deeper way. It's an ongoing unfolding that is a joy and an honor to take part in and that makes all the hard work we do in order to help others with our gifts truly fulfilling.

THREE TRAITS TO GUIDE YOU FROM HERE

In order to help you stay on the path of living into your "meant for more," it helps to have a few guiding principles that will keep you on track and in alignment with being a force for good and a leader in your own life and in the lives of others. Generosity, courage, and compassion are those principles. These traits form a three-legged stool—you need each one of them to keep yourself upright and stable on your never-ending journey to more.

- **Generosity.** When you think of the word *generosity*, you likely think of things like giving to charity, or giving gifts to loved ones, or perhaps being quick to share a compliment. While these are all lovely and important things to do, the generosity that will help you make your version of "more" a reality is giving for the sake of opening up a possibility for someone else. You want to make your offer and lead your life with a generosity of spirit. Coming from generosity can also help you get past the concern that you're bragging or being too full of yourself when offering your expertise.

  I take inspiration from the George Bernard Shaw quote that says, "This is the true joy in life, the being used for a purpose recognized by yourself as a mighty one." Generously give yourself over to your purpose, and you will experience true joy.

There's also an element to generosity that pertains to giving to yourself, as well: You're giving yourself a chance to become the person and the leader you know you're capable of becoming, and making the difference you feel in your bones you're here to make. Giving yourself the chance to step into leadership and open others' minds to new possibilities creates an upward spiral. It's how you lift as you climb—it benefits everyone, including you.

- **Courage.** It takes courage to turn your generosity into something tangible; it's what gets you to open your mouth and make your offer. It takes courage to believe that your gifts are valuable, and to be generous with those gifts. I hope it will help you to know that the word *courage* is derived from the Latin word for heart—it's not about having an iron will; it's about leading with love.

    It's a courageous act to step into all of who you are and to acknowledge that you want more for yourself, for other people, and for the world, even though you are already so blessed. Courage is what helps you acknowledge that you're ready to break through in those moments when you can sense that you've outgrown your current container. It helps you let go of who you've become for the possibility of who you can be.

- **Compassion.** The definition of empathy is being able to identify with another's experience. (Think of Bill Clinton's famous line, "I feel your pain." That's empathy.) Compassion takes empathy one step further— you can put yourself in someone else's shoes *and* you have a desire to reduce their suffering.

Compassion is what happens when you take the time to listen to someone's dreams, desires, and visions. It's what spurs you to offer them a new possibility. Like generosity, compassion also cuts two ways: Your compassion for the people who are experiencing a pain that you know you can help them with spurs your generosity to make an offer. And your compassion for yourself empowers you to acknowledge your own pain of knowing you're meant for more and not living it yet. It spurs you to give yourself the chance to feel truly fulfilled, and do it in a way that doesn't make you feel overworked or taken advantage of.

When it comes to living into your "meant for more," it takes all three of these traits. Without courage, you might not ever make your offer. Without generosity, you might keep your efforts on a surface level where they don't have as much impact. And without compassion, you might give advice that doesn't truly serve others; you might also work yourself into the ground trying to help others if you don't have compassion for yourself.

If you ever feel stuck on your journey to uncovering your "meant for more," ask yourself, *Where can I be more generous, courageous, or compassionate?* These three touchstones will get you back on track to making the difference that you are uniquely able to provide.

This quote from Theodore Roosevelt (which I was introduced to via Brené Brown's wonderful book *Daring Greatly*) always does the job of reminding me why it's important to our souls that we unwrap our gifts and share them with the world:

"It is not the critic who counts; not the man who points out how the strong man stumbles, or where the doer of deeds could have done them better. The credit belongs to the man who is actually in the arena, whose face is marred by dust and sweat and blood; who strives valiantly; who errs, who comes short again and again, because there is no effort without error and shortcoming; but who does actually strive to do the deeds; who knows great enthusiasms, the great devotions; who spends himself in a worthy cause; who at the best knows in the end the triumph of high achievement, and who at the worst, if he fails, at least fails while daring greatly. . . ."

For some people, the journey itself is the reward; for others, both the journey and the rewards are equally important. I fall into the latter category—I enjoy the journey *and* I want the rewards. There are both kinds of people, and one isn't better or more right than the other. Whatever rewards you want for yourself, remember that they are a natural and just consequence to getting out there with your gifts and helping the people you were meant to help. Enjoy them. You deserve them!

KICK-START YOUR "MORE" WITH A 30-DAY MEANT FOR MORE CHALLENGE

I know that I have thrown a lot of information, exercises, and—I hope—inspiration at you in these pages. To make it truly transformational, you have to do two things: 1) Admit that you are ready to step into your "meant for more," and 2) take consistent action in the direction of your "more."

I've given you as much as I can pack into the pages of this book to empower you and entice you into deciding that you are, indeed, meant for more. Now the actual decision is in your hands. Will you say yes to yourself?

Where I can still help once you've made the decision to walk the path to discover your "more," is with the second part of that equation: taking action. To make it as simple and clear as possible, I've organized everything I covered in this book into a 30-day challenge that will help get you into action and help you keep track of what you've done, what's still to come, and where you are in the process.

All the information you need to complete the challenge is currently in your hands, but you can also get additional support and inspiration by joining me and my team at www. MeantForMoreBook.com/Facebook. We will be waiting to greet you and cheer you on, so come join us!

First 7 Days: Make Peace with Sales

Like many people, it's possible you've got a lifetime of negative thoughts and associations with sales. The good news is you can go a long way toward rewriting those narratives by spending one week challenging yourself to think and act differently and start imagining new possibilities. To do that, aim to complete these five tasks in the first seven days:

- Uncover your hidden beliefs about selling using the exercise in Chapter 1.

- Make a list of all the ways you are already selling in your own life.

- Write a new definition of sales for yourself following the instructions in Chapter 1.

- Use the Active Imagination exercise in Chapter 2 to name your desires.

- Get clear on the good you can do in the world by doing the Calculate Your Ripple exercise in Chapter 3.

Reminder: All worksheets mentioned above can be downloaded at www.MeantForMoreGuide.com.

Days 8–18: Claim Your Gifts and Get into Action

Because Step Two of the Meant for More Formula is so packed with actual actions, I'm going to give you 10 days to complete these next steps. I think you'll find, though, that the more actions you take, the more momentum you create, so trust that once you start moving, you'll uncover energy that propels you along.

- Uncover your gifts by completing at least one of the exercises in Chapter 4: look to your life story, see where you meddle, or think about the people you've helped.

- Take at least one step to create an opportunity where you can share your gifts with more than one person. Make a list of 10 places where the people you aim to help are gathering (using the worksheet I reference in Chapter 4), put together a simple summary of what you want to talk or teach about, and/or book a room and post an invite on Facebook!

- Give yourself an expert title using the exercise in Chapter 5; for extra credit, have a business card printed up with your new title on it or update your website or social media profile with it.

- At least twice during these 10 days, do a Daily Stretch, following the guidelines in Chapter 6.

- Spend at least one hour, or as much as a whole morning or afternoon, closing open loops (use the exercise in Chapter 7 as inspiration).

- Complete the Best Next Move exercise in Chapter 8 at least three times.

Days 19–26: Inspire Others with Your Irresistible Offer

This next week is all about crafting your offer. This is the grain of sand around which I've built my entire business—taking the time to really put some good thought into how you want to invite people to take action is one of the most important things you can do to set yourself up for success. You can always refine your offer as you go, but you've got to start somewhere. So please don't skip this part!

- Complete the Unique Offer Identifier exercise in Chapter 9 to help you find the words to describe what you do in a way that will prompt your ideal client to really open up and hear you.

- Use the exercise in Chapter 9 to uncover your Unique Branded System for helping others.

- Determine what bonuses and limiters you'll use to create tension, inspire on-the-spot action, and invite pursuit.

- Write up a one- or two-paragraph intro for yourself that incorporates a bit of your personal story as well as your credentials.

- Reach out to a handful of people you've helped in the past and ask them for a testimonial so that you have social proof that your unique gift is of value to others.

- Make your offer to at least one person this week, even if it's just to a friend and just for practice.

Days 27–30: Live Your More

In these last few days of this life-changing month, it's time to give yourself some tools to help you stay the course. This is where you turn a 30-day challenge into a lifestyle that supports you over the long term.

- Start a tradition of writing down or verbally sharing three wins each day.

- Commit to some structure—a class, an accountability partner, a mastermind program, or other group—that will keep you on track.

- Give some thought to your current circle of friends. Are there relationships you need to let go of so that you can be more inspired, or are there people who inspire you whom you can reach out to and forge a deeper relationship with?

- Write out a short letter or note to yourself, giving yourself permission to pursue your "meant for more."

- Tithe 10 percent of everything you earn in the next 30 days to people, places, or institutions that feed you spiritually—and let the rewards you receive help you decide if you continue tithing for the next six months.

Remember, you don't have to do this 30-day challenge on your own. My team and I—along with everyone else who reads this book and commits to taking this challenge—will be on our Facebook group, sharing tips, inspiration, and camaraderie. Come join us by visiting www.MeantForMoreBook.com/Facebook and let us support you!

Now you have the formula to live your "meant for more," and to make your unique version of "more" a reality. You have the inspiration. You have the information. Now it's time to claim your "more," and enjoy the transformation that comes from living your gifts. The world needs that something special that only you can offer!

POSTSCRIPT

When you've got a good life, you're healthy, your kids are doing well, and there's nothing to "complain" about, it can be harder to uplevel than when it's obvious that things are falling apart. We've all heard the saying that good is the enemy of great. I believe it.

Writing this book—and turning 50, which happened while I was writing it—has caused me to evaluate my own life and all the places where I can live my own "meant for more" at a higher level.

The truth is, living into this book has turned my life inside out, in a really good way. I'm still between the trapezes, but so many important things have happened since I started writing. For starters, I completed a romantic relationship that—while spicy and exciting—was not growing in the direction of my "meant for more." God has already blessed me with new connections to earth angels who are walking a more congruent path of contribution, generosity, and courage.

I've upped my inner work, personal development, and spirituality, which I haven't done at this level in a while. I feel reconnected to my own generosity, courage, and compassion, and I feel more alive than ever.

I've realized that my "meant for more" now is about empowering leaders to live their "meant for more." As such, I restructured my company and gave myself some creative white space to step into being able to serve you, our Meant for More tribe, in an even more meaningful way.

Overall I feel more present and connected and fulfilled than I have in a long time. I'm delighted, but I'm not surprised. This is what happens when you allow your "meant for more" to come to life. It's sometimes a bumpy ride, but it's all in service of bringing the biggest version of you to life.

I'm honored to have you here, right now, during what I like to think of as our divine appointment, and to provide that space to stretch that your soul has been longing for.

In some ways it's a selfish act on my part.

You see, it's now clearer to me than ever before that I would implode without you. And that's what it feels like when you tap into your "meant for more." You can't not do it. You can't not give it. You can't not live it.

Welcome to your new life. I'm honored to walk this path with you.

RECOMMENDED READING

Below are the books I've mentioned throughout this book, titles that have inspired me personally and that I have shared again and again with clients. I trust they will move you, too.

The Little Me and the Great Me by Lou Austin

True Purpose by Tim Kelly

Conversations with God by Neale Donald Walsh

You^2 by Price Pritchett

The Four Spiritual Laws of Prosperity by Edwene Gaines

Daring Greatly by Brene Brown

Think and Grow Rich by Napoleon Hill

ACKNOWLEDGMENTS

There's something special about each and every one of us, and deep down inside we know it. The magic happens when we take the opportunity to share that gift with another person. I'm honored to have this chance to thank the people who touched my life with their gifts and inspired me to live my "meant for more."

Heavenly gratitude to my mom, Ina Garson, and my dad, Eddie Garson, who lived their lives with passion, stayed connected post-divorce, and always made me feel that I could do anything I set my mind to. Thank you for modeling the importance of imperfect parenting that puts connection first. I'm deeply grateful for my connection with my brilliant, beautiful, creative teens, Elijah and Sierra, who make all of the hard parts worth it and inspire me every day.

Deep praise for their father, Michael Sasevich, who always believed in me and showed me the true meaning of the motto "Never give up."

I would not be who I am today without the following mentors and organizations that shaped my mind-set and thus my path. Never-ending gratitude to The Landmark Forum and the person who had the courage to introduce me to their classes shortly after I lost my mother when I was 19. Learning that I could create my life versus believing that I would be stuck with the one I was handed changed everything. From there I encountered More University. For nearly 30 years, their incredible work on sensuality and alternative lifestyles has shaped this great life adventure I get to live.

I'm forever thankful to Alison Armstrong, founder of PAX Programs, Inc., for her commitment to heaven on earth and peace between men and women. To this day your work shapes my life. Thank you for knowing that I needed to discover my own path. I love and appreciate you so much and always will.

Thanks to Edwene Gaines who stood on the stage at Agape Spiritual Center on Mother's Day, 2005, and introduced me to the difference tithing could make in my life. To this day it is the secret sauce of my fulfillment and abundance.

Thank you, JJ Virgin, for knowing it was time for me to write this book and for the stand you continue to take for me to have the best life ever. And to my agent, Celeste Fine, for your enthusiasm and immediate yes to the idea . . . before I could get cold feet!

It has been my lifelong dream to be published by Hay House. Because of Hay House I was exposed to Marianne Williamson's *Return to Love* (via cassette tape!) in my early 20s. I remember thinking, "Wow! My deepest fear is not that I'm inadequate, it's that I'm powerful beyond measure. How does she know? This is incredible!" Thank you for all the ways you've gone first, Marianne. And the same to Mary Morrissey and your incredible mentorship and love as you've helped me through painful times and directed me toward my dreams.

Thank you, Kate Hanley, for taking my spoken words and my heart and organizing them into this beautiful book. And for getting so into our work that you became a student, a truly special moment for me. It's no surprise that you named this book. You put a name to what I see when I look in our students' eyes, and I'm forever grateful.

And speaking of my students, wow! Thank you to the nearly 1,000 Sales, Authenticity & Success Mastermind alumni who proved the effectiveness of our awesome sales structures over and over with their own work. And our over 15,000 students around the world who make a bigger difference because you learned from us. We call this book "The Proven Formula to Turn Your Knowledge into Profits" because of YOU! I'm also so grateful for our clients who contributed their inspiring stories and personal lessons to this book so we could all benefit from their experiences and insights.

And last but not least, deep gratitude to each and every member of The Invisible Close team who served by my side over the last decade and made all of my dreams and visions come true. Thank you, Andrea Almaraz, for your enthusiastic daily yes to our mission and for your compassionate, loving leadership and friendship. And Lisa Cherney for being my go-to spiritual advisor, biggest fan, bestie, and the most awesome co-leader I could ever hope for. And thank you to Andrea J. Lee for showing up on our leadership team at exactly the right times and helping us innovate in ways that fed everything and caused our business, and my heart, to grow.

Thank you, Stacey Lievens, for making me look and feel feminine and powerful in the thousands of wonderful photos you took and in all our interactions as lifelong friends. Your generous heart is a gift to this world. And to Peggy Murrah and Angela Spisak who, to this day, support me and this work behind the scenes, making so much of what we do online and how we care for our clients possible in an ongoing, heartfelt way. To Erin Tillotson for helping me empower entrepreneurs across the globe, year after year, with our social media and podcast offerings. We sure love to give!

And my deepest gratitude to my financial team of angels— Siliva Saunders, Sharon Losnick and Orin Green—who root me on, encourage me to go for it, inspire me to continue to be generous, and provide me with the feeling of confidence I need to keep swinging for the fences as I take inspired, imperfect action over and over again.

Cheers to everything that led up to now and the opportunity you have all given me to live my meant for more. May you continue to do the same, with all of your heart.

ABOUT THE AUTHOR

"There's something special about you, and deep down inside you know it. Now it's time to let the world know it too. Yes, you can stand out and make a difference in this increasingly noisy world. You are truly Meant for More!"

— LISA SASEVICH

After helping corporate giants like Pfizer and Hewlett-Packard generate millions in sales and small personal development companies quickly grow their annual revenue from six to seven figures, **Lisa Sasevich** was fired from her dream job the night before Christmas Eve. With a husband in medical school and two toddlers at home, it was devastating.

After some soul-searching, the "Queen of Sales Conversion" decided it was time to parlay her talents into her own profits – and to help others do the same. She started a home-based business with nothing more than her phone, her laptop and the stolen hours of the night after her kids were tucked into bed.

A few short years and over $40 million in sales later, Lisa has helped over 15,000 thousand clients in 134 countries earn more by doing what they love, all without being pushy or salesy. Lisa's company, The Invisible Close™, has been honored to be in the *Inc.* 500 and named one of *Inc.* magazine's fastest-growing privately held companies two years in a row, #20 in woman-owned businesses.

Her mission: To help people make the difference they know they were put here to make, *and* to make great money doing it.

Lisa lives in San Diego, where she loves seeing her teenage son Elijah and daughter Sierra enjoy new, life-expanding experiences (as long as she picks them out and closely supervises). **www.LisaSasevich.com**

START LIVING YOUR

MEANT FOR MORE

TODAY!

I hope you've enjoyed reading this book and learned all you can during our time together!

Keep this momentum going and head over to MeantForMoreGuide.com to download your FREE companion workbook.

With the Meant for More Formula and workbook combined, you too can make big money and a big difference doing what you love—and now you don't need to go at it alone.

Thousands of experts, service professionals, coaches, and mission-driven entrepreneurs from around the world have used my proven systems to create a life and business they love.

Visit LisaSasevich.com to learn more about my popular home-study programs, designed to help you craft and make your irresistible offer with confidence—all without being pushy or sales-y.

Finally, I invite you to connect with me on social media for more content and to join the Meant for More community. You can find me on LinkedIn, Facebook, Twitter, Instagram, and YouTube @LisaSasevich.

To your success!

Lisa Sasevich

Whether you're just getting started or ready to grow, we have a program that's right for you at www.LisaSasevich.com. Here's a few favorites!

NAIL YOUR *Lisa Sasevich* OFFER SYSTEM

Clarify, Package, Price & Deliver Your Irresistible Offer

Your offer is everything. It's your business. It's your life. Your offer combined with your Unique Branded System™ (UBS) are two of the most powerful tools you can have. Clarity on your offer is the first step in maximizing your profits. If you feel stuck or struggle to find the words to say what you do in a clear and compelling way, the Nail Your Offer System will give you the foundation you need to create an offer that finally says exactly what you do. Your offer will be clear, concise, and irresistible—meaning your ideal clients will never feel sold to, just served… and you'll be set up to get results fast.

SPEAK-TO-SELL
BOOTCAMP

Craft Your Signature Talk & Get Gigs

The Speak-to-Sell Formula teaches you exactly how to tell your story, craft your irresistible offer and make your offer from live and virtual stages in the most authentic way. Don't let the words "speaking" or "selling" scare you. This system provides the structure to effortlessly make your offer—even if you've never viewed yourself as a salesperson. Yes, you can get on stage with confidence, teach and give, and still hit the markers that inspire an on-the-spot yes to working with, or booking a consultation with, you!

HAY HOUSE TITLES
OF RELATED INTEREST

YOU CAN HEAL YOUR LIFE, the movie,
starring Louise Hay & Friends
(available as a 1-DVD programme, an expanded 2-DVD set
and an online streaming video)
Learn more at www.hayhouse.com/louise-movie

THE SHIFT, the movie,
starring Dr Wayne W. Dyer
(available as a 1-DVD programme, an expanded 2-DVD set
and an online streaming video)
Learn more at www.hayhouse.com/the-shift-movie

• • •

*CHILLPRENEUR: The New Rules for Creating Success, Freedom, and
Abundance on Your Own Terms,* by Denise Duffield-Thomas

*CHOOSE: The Single Most Important Decision before Starting
Your Business,* by Ryan Levesque

*OVERDELIVER: Build a Business for a Lifetime Playing the Long Game
in Direct Response Marketing,* by Brian Kurtz

WORTHY: Boost Your Self-Worth to Grow Your Net Worth,
by Nancy Levin

All of the above are available at www.hayhouse.co.uk

• • •

Listen. Learn. Transform.

Listen to the audio version of this book for FREE!

Gain access to powerful tools and life-changing insights from world-renowned experts—guiding and inspiring you as you work toward your goals. With the *Hay House Unlimited* Audio app, you can learn and grow in a way that fits your lifestyle . . . and your daily schedule.

With your membership, you can:

- Learn how to take your writing to the next level, start and build your business, and create abundance in all areas of your life.

- Explore thousands of audiobooks, meditations, immersive learning programs, podcasts, and more.

- Access exclusive audios you won't find anywhere else.

- Experience completely unlimited listening. No credits. No limits. No kidding.

Try for FREE!

Hay House Podcasts
Bring Fresh, Free Inspiration Each Week!

Hay House proudly offers a selection of life-changing audio content via our most popular podcasts!

Hay House Meditations Podcast

Features your favorite Hay House authors guiding you through meditations designed to help you relax and rejuvenate. Take their words into your soul and cruise through the week!

Dr. Wayne W. Dyer Podcast

Discover the timeless wisdom of Dr. Wayne W. Dyer, world-renowned spiritual teacher and affectionately known as "the father of motivation." Each week brings some of the best selections from the 10-year span of Dr. Dyer's talk show on Hay House Radio.

Hay House Podcast

Enjoy a selection of insightful and inspiring lectures from Hay House Live events, listen to some of the best moments from previous Hay House Radio episodes, and tune in for exclusive interviews and behind-the-scenes audio segments featuring leading experts in the fields of alternative health, self-development, intuitive medicine, success, and more! Get motivated to live your best life possible by subscribing to the free Hay House Podcast.

Find Hay House podcasts on iTunes, or visit
www.HayHouse.com/podcasts for more info.

HAY HOUSE

Look within

Join the conversation about latest products,
events, exclusive offers and more.

   Hay House

   @HayHouseUK

   @hayhouseuk

We'd love to hear from you!